THE
SOUL
OF
BRASIL

THE
SOUL
OF
BRASIL

BY
ANISTATIA MILLER & JARED BROWN

Sagatiba

puro espírito do brasil[®]

THE
SOUL
OF
BRAZIL

4

Cover and interior book design: Anistatia Miller

Cover photograph plus images on pages 8, 102, 113, 14, 117, 132, 144, 147, 149, and 159: © 2007 Jared Brown

First printing

TABLE OF CONTENTS

Foreword by Marcos Moraes • 6

PART ONE: IN THE BEGINNING • 9

Chapter One: The Silk Route • 11

Chapter Two: The New World • 33

Chapter Three: Mother Portugal Discovers Cachaça • 56

Chapter Four: The Decline of Cachaça • 70

Chapter Five: Brasil Rediscovers Its Heart & Spirit • 80

PART TWO: THE ANATOMY OF CACHAÇA • 101

Chapter Six: The Heartof Cachaça • 103

Chapter Seven: What Is Cachaça • 109

Chapter Eight: Tasting Cachaça • 133

Chapter Nine: Classic Cachaça Drinks • 145

Chapter Ten: Cachaça Food • 157

Chapter Eleven: Cachaça Today • 164

Chapter Twelve: Sagatiba's Role
in Cachaça's Recent History • 168

Appendix: Regional Names & Euphemisms
for Cachaça • 173

Index • 179

About the Authors • 184

FOREWORD

I AM BRASILIAN, and as with all Brasilians, I take cachaça seriously. Cachaça is more than the national spirit of Brasil, it exemplifies our national spirt. Brasilians enjoy cachaça in caiparinhas or aged cachaças as aperitifs or after-dinner drinks. While I appreciate fine wine, cognac, absinthe and other fine spirits, nothing captures the magic of Brasil and elicits memories of good times with friends and a spectacular beach like the caipirinha. It is a magnificent cocktail packed with great memories.

While I was on vacation in the Mediterranean I was shocked to find people were drinking caipirinhas made with very rough, low quality cachaça and sometimes even vodka. It dawned on me that people around the world would only experience a caipirinha if it were made from the kinds of premium cachaças only found in Brasil. As I left to return home I decided that I was going to show the world what superb cachaça is about…Sagatiba Pura was born.

Next, together with our master distiller we went on to identify wonderful aged cachaças which are ideal for sipping. I simply could not believe it when we found an amazing cache of the best cachaça I or anyone I know had ever tasted, forgotten for more than twenty-three years, aging in nineteenth-century French oak barrels at the oldest mill in São Paulo.

That, by the way, is a perfect example of the endless stories about cachaça which we would love to share with you. As you will see in this book, the variety of cachaça is vast, and cachaça's history is the history of Brasil. I hope that your journey of discovering them is as wonderful as mine has been.

Saude!

Marcos Moraes
Founder and President
Sagatiba

IN THE BEGINNING

The Silk Route

A BRIEF HISTORY OF DISTILLATION

"Eau-de-vie is an element newly revealed to man,
but hid from antiquity because the human race
was then too young to need this beverage
which was destined to revive the energies of
modern decrepitude."
—Ramon Llull (circa 1232–1316 AD)

PATRICK MCGOVERN, an archaeochemist from the Museum of Applied Science Center for Archaeology, discovered clues to the truth of Medieval alchemist Ramon Llull's statement when he and a team of Chinese archaeologists uncovered vessels containing traces of a beverage fermented from rice, honey, and fruit in the Neolithic, northern Chinese village of Jiaju that date back to circa 7000 BC: about the time

PAGE OPPOSITE:
An example of an
early Chinese still.

cultures in the Near East were brewing up and storing barley beer and wild grape wine. But then McGovern has been excavating all sorts of interesting finds like this for about a decade now. He has uncoverd tightly-lidded bronze vessels from the Shang and Western Zhou dynasties (circa 1250–1000 BC) in Anyang, China, filled with aromatized rice and millet wines macerated with wormwood, chrysanthemum, China fir, elemi, and other herbs and flowers, just like the ones described in a few Shang dynasty oracle-bone inscriptions.[1] (For some of you, this formula may sound a bit like a precursor to Hippocratic wine— a concoction of wormwood, dittany, and sweet wine—and its more famous descendant vermouth—wine, wormwood, plus a bunch of other herbs and spices.)

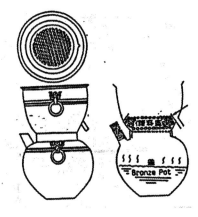

A Chinese still from the early Han Dynasty (circa 250 AD).

And although the academic jury is still out on his postulation that viniculture has its origins in Eurasia, before spreading south and west, McGovern did present hardcore evidence that wine was made in Shulaveri, Georgia (circa 6000 BC); in the Haji Firuz Tepe, Iran (circa 5400–5000 BC); and in Late Uruk, Mesopotamia (circa 3500–3100 BC) in his book *Ancient Wine: The Search for the Origins of*

---

1   For more details on this subject, see David N. Keightley's *Sources of Shang History: The Oracle-Bone Inscriptions of Bronze Age China.* (Berkeley: University of California Press, 1978).

Viniculture (Princeton: Princeton University Press, 2003).

But enough about wine and beer. We're here to muse on more potent potables. We're here to talk about distilled alcohol and what people have done with it over the ages.

L ET'S START with the origin of the word. Alcohol has been said to come from the Arabic term *al kohl,* meaning "powder of antimony," the stuff that women in the eastern hemisphere used to darken their eyelids: the world's first eye shadow. This powder was produced through the distillation of stibinite, a natural sulfide of the metalloid antimony. Eventually the term was broadened to describe the essence of any material.[2] Despite the logic of this oft-repeated history, it is more likely that the word originates from the Arabic word *al kol,* or *al ghol* which old Arab texts defined as "1: a genie or spirit that takes on varied shapes (a supernatural creature in Arab mythology). 2: Any drug or substance that takes away the mind

al kol

1: a genie or spirit that takes on varied shapes.

2: Any drug or substance that takes away the mind or covers it.

---

2   Harold McGee narrated a concise history of alcohol in chapter 9 of his book *On Food and Cooking: The Science and Lore of the Kitchen* (New York: Fireside, 1984).

or covers it."[3] However, distilling predates this term, and the word itself may have been introduced into Arabic culture from India.

Now let's go back in time a few steps.

About 9,000 years ago, the Chinese distilled essences of plant, animal, and mineral matter to make medicines and perfumes by capturing the vapors of the boiled ingredients with a catch-bowl, which was connected by a side-tube to a receiver. The Mongols, on the other hand, used a rudimentary method commonly known as freeze distillation to produce *arkhi* from mare's milk. They allowed the water in the fermented milk to freeze. Then they removed the low-alcohol solids to bring the alcohol concentration as high as thirty percent. (Early American settlers used this same method in frigid New England to make applejack. However, it is not recommended as it also concentrates methyl alcohol and other congeners in the solution, unlike distillation by heat.)

Neighboring nations picked up on the process as the Chinese established trade routes by land along the Silk Road and by sea, connecting them to India, Persia, Egypt, and every place in between beginning somewhere between 3500 and 3000 BC. In addition to silk and spices, most of the world's body of civilized knowledge was transmitted and adapted along these two routes. Noodle making, astrology, printing, and especially alchemy (a study that com-

3   Hajar, Rachel, MD, FACC, "Alcohol: Friend of Foe, A Historical Perspective," *Heart Views*, Vol. 1, No. 9, September -November 2000: 341-344.

bined physics, medicine, astrology, semiotics, mysticism, spiritualism, chemistry, metallurgy, and art into one big package) were valuable commodities.

How do we know this information was shared? Here's one example: In the Vedas, *somarasa* (meaning "liquor") was the drink of the gods that made them immortal. A ritual intoxicant associated with Indra (the god of weather and war as well as chief deity), *somarasa* was derived from the somalatha plant and consumed during religious festivals, especially the Somayajnas: *atyanistama, uktya, sodasi, vajapeya, atiratra*, and *aptoryama*.

Considered to be the oldest surviving written texts, the Vedas were originally written in Sanskrit beginning in 2500 BC.[4] Based on this piece of evidence, the Chinese and Proto-Indo-Iranians (formerly called Aryans of India) exchanged ideas and goods for about a thousand years by then.

As the Proto-Indo Iranians' civilization morphed into Hindu culture, the Vedas—and the culture's body of knowledge—expanded considerably. In Kautilya's *Arthasastra*, a treatise on governing and economic policy written circa 500 BC, a number of liquors are mentioned, including *medaka, prasanna, asava* (made from cereals, fruits, roots, barks, flowers, or sugar cane), *arita, maireya*, and *madhu*. And in the *Susruta-Samhita*, the second of two volumes on ayurvedic medicine written circa

---

4   This is discussed in lengthy detail with citations in "Indian Chemistry through the Ages" by D.P. Agrawal (http://www.infinityfoundation.com/mandala/t_es/t_es_agraw_chemistry.htm).

100 BC, uses the word *khola* is used to describe alcoholic beverages.

From archaeological evidence discovered in northern India's Ganharan cities of Taxila[5] and Charsadda,[6] the design of stills used for the extraction of alcohol (as opposed to mercury or other essences) was greatly refined by 150 BC.[7]

By this time, of course, basic information about distillation had traveled back to Greece after Alexander the Great[8] conquered the Persian Empire (which included Anatolia, Syria, Phoenicia, Gaza, Egypt, Bactria, and Mesopotamia) and invaded northern India up to the border of the Punjab by 326 BC, about twenty-five years too late for one Greek scholar.

It is doubtful that much if any information on the finer points of distilling reached Aristotle, who wrote in his 350 BC work *Meteorology*:

> "Salt water when it turns into vapour becomes sweet, and the vapour does not form salt water when it condenses again. This I know by experiment. The same thing is true in every case of the kind: wine and all fluids that evaporate and con-

---

5   The city was situated on a major junction where the main trade routes of the Silk Road, the royal highway from Pataliputra in the northwest via Bactria, and the route from Kashmir and Central Asia all converge.

6   The city is located in what is now a northwest frontier province of Pakistan.

7   Needham, Joseph. *Science and Civilisation in China*. Vols. IV (2), V(4). (Cambridge: Cambridge University Press).

8   It is interesting to note that Alexander the Great's wife Roxana was from Bactria (now Afghanistan), a country that regularly traded with India at the city of Taxila.

dense back into a liquid state become water. They all are water modified by a certain admixture, the nature of which determines their flavour. But this subject must be considered on another more suitable occasion."[9]

In this early documentation of distillation in Greece, Aristotle demonstrated a reasonable proficiency with a rudimentary still, but no knowledge that he had created something far more interesting than water from wine. (A few hundred years later, both Hypathia and Zosimos of Alexandria proposed the four basic elements—fire, earth, air, and water—could be transmutated through distillation around 300 AD. But even they did not delve deeper into the secrets of collecting essences.)

The Indian distillation process made its way to Egypt via Ptolemy I Soter, one of Alexander's Macedonian generals who had accompanied him to India before being sent to rule Egypt. As pharaoh, Ptolemy established Egypt's Hellenic dynasty in 323 BC as well as the greatest library of written knowledge in ancient times, the Alexandrian Library, an annex to the Hall of the Muses. Scholars from every corner of the civilized world conducted

Aristotle was one of the first westerners to muse on the potential of distillation.

9   Aristolte. *Meteorology*. Webster, E. W., translator (The Internet Classic Archive, 2000).

research at this spectacular repository for the next four to six centuries. That is, until Roman emperor Diocletian ordered the burning of the alchemists' manuscripts in 296 AD to safeguard his economy. After all, alchemists were trying to turn lead into gold and his economy was based on a finite supply of this precious metal. Christian monks sacked the remaining contents in 389 AD because Greek, Arabic, and Aramaic were pagan languages as far as they were concerned and therefore taboo. Thus a few centuries of pooled knowledge went up in smoke.

However, as Christianity never took hold in Arabia or Persia, the book-burners were not entirely successful. The Alexandrian Library's contents were merely copies. The originals had been returned to their respective Arab, Indian, Greek, Hebrew, and Nabatean owners after careful transcription. Anyone who could still read those languages after Latin was deemed Europe's scholarly tongue could continue to do research, reading behind closed doors or traveling great distances.

Budding pharmacologists found copies of Greek physician Pedanius Dioscorides' *De Materia Media* (the basis for pharmacology for nearly 1,500 years after its publication in the First Century AD) and learned how to distill and administer turpentine as a medicine. (Dioscorides' still was rudimentary: a clay vase covered with several layers of wool, suspended on a wooden rack over a fire. The distillate was collected by squeezing the collected vapors out of the fibers.[10])

The Arab Alchemists

NEXT PERSON in the distillation puzzle was Abu Musa Jabir Hayyan (aka: Geber or Jabir, the "father of Arab chemistry"), who lived in Persia during the 700s AD. Besides being a basic all-around alchemist (meaning he was a pharmacist, philosopher, astronomer, and physicist), Geber was methodical to the core, stressing the importance of systemized experimentation. He systematically distilled and consequently discovered hydrochloric acid, sulphiric acid, nitric acid, acetic acid, tartaric acid, and citric acid, using a fascinating little invention called the *taqtir*

The father of Arab chemistry Geber created the world's first alembic still.

---

10   See the discussion of distilled waters in Liliane Plouvier's *L'Europe se Met à Table: Multiculturalité, identité européenne et habitudes alimentaires* (Brussels: DG Education et Culture, Initiative Connect lancée par la Commission européenne et le Parlement européen, 2000).

or alembic still and jotting down his findings in his *Kitab ikhraj ma fe al-quwwa ila al-fi'l:*[11]

> "And fire which burns on the mouths of bottles due to boiled wine and salt, and similar things with nice characteristics which are thought to be of little use, these are of great significance in these sciences."

Of course, the raw distillate wasn't much good for drinking, but one thing is certain. Al-Geber's experiments with the distillation of ethanol from wine planted the seed of inspiration in the minds of Abu Bakr Muhammad ibn Zakariya Razi (aka: al-Razi or Rhazes; 865-925 AD), who went on to perfect the process for making beverage alcohol, and Abu Yusuf Ya'qub ibn Ishaq al-Kindi who offered up 107 formulas plus a still design in his treatise *Kitab Kimya Al-'Itr wa Al Tas'idat.*

"And fire which burns on the mouths of bottles due to boiled wine...these are of great significance in these sciences."

By this time, the Moors had already invaded the Iberian Peninsula, staying from 711 until 1200 AD. With them, they brought many of the trappings of Islamic science: the city of Cordoba had public baths, air-conditioned and heated buildings, street lights, perfumes, distillates made from wine, and a pile of lovely books that explained how to make them.

Under Pope Sylvester II (died 1003 AD), western society was introduced to Arab astronomy and

11   This treatise was included in *Mukhtarat rasa'il Jabir ibn Hayyan* edited by P. Kraus (Cairo: 1935, p.76).

mathematics, and Arabic numerals in place of the clumsy Roman ones. Christian monks and scholars managed to keep a dialogue running about their scientific studies and findings during this Muslim occupation of Spain and set themselves to the arduous task of translating more Arabic works into Latin. Robert of Chester, who lived in Segovia, was one of them. In 1144, he finished translating many of Geber's, Al-Kindi's, and Al-Razi's findings on distillation from Arabic to Latin in his *Liber de Compositione Alchimae*.[12]

Aqua Vitae Is Born

Arnaud de Ville-Neuve

BOOKS like Robert of Chester's made their way into the hands of scholars in Catalonia during the late 1200s including Arnaud de Ville-Neuve (circa 1235–1313),[13] who was the first European alchemist to document the distillation of wine for consumption. He is also credited with coining the phrases *aqua*

---

12 Holmyard, Eric John, *Makers of Chemistry*, (Oxford: Oxford University Press, 1931) p. 86.

13 Also known as Arnaldus de Villa Nova, Arnaldus de Villanueva, Arnaldus Villanovanus, Arnaud de Villeneuve or Arnau de Vilanova, this alchemist was also possibly born in Languedoc Ville-Neuve-the-Maguelone in what was then the kingdom of Aragon.

vitae and *eau-de-vie* (meaning "water of life" in Latin and in French, respectively).

Both Spain and France claim de Ville-Neuve to be a native son. The Spanish say he was born in the Catalan village of Villaneuva, while the French declare Villeneuve-Loubet near Nice to be his birth home.

What is known of his early life is that he began his education in Barcelona under the tutelage of John Casamila, a celebrated professor of medicine. There, de Ville-Neuve found himself attracted to the discoveries of Claudius Galen (129–216 AD) and al-Razi (865–925 AD), who had significantly advanced the process for making beverage alcohol.

At the height of his career, de Ville-Neuve was regarded as the age's best physician and alchemist, attending to the health of popes Innocent V, Boniface VIII, Benedict IX, and Clement V as well as monarchs Pedro III and James II of Aragon, Robert of Naples, and Frederick II of Sicily. He even served as vice-chancellor of the eminent University of Montpellier, while teaching medicine, botany, and alchemy.

The father of European distillation Arnaud de Ville-Neuve is also credited with inventing armagnac.

But in his later years, his life more closely resembled that of al-Kindi. While he focused more on research, his fame garnered ecclesiastic and academic enmity. Both the Spanish and Parisian Inquisitions exiled him to Sicily for his views on the mass, the Antichrist, Jesus Christ, and Armageddon. But his skills could not be denied. While in asylum, in 1313, an ailing Pope Clement V called upon de Ville-Neuve to tend to him. Sadly, de Ville-Neuve died near Genoa on the voyage.

Like his Arab predecessors, de Ville-Neuve wrote numerous treatises, twenty-one of them in all. It is his 1310 book *Liber de Vinis* ("The Book of Wine") that he proclaimed his discovery of the long-sought universal panacea to prolong life: the water of life, the fountain of youth. He mentioned *aqua vine* ("water of wine"), commenting that "some name it *aqua vitae*." The book was a bestseller and the term stuck.

"...some name it aqua vitae..."

Some historians say de Ville-Neuve also discovered or perfected the mutage process: fortifying wine with spirits to halt fermentation and preserve sweetness. He is further credited with the invention of armagnac.

By the time de Ville-Neuve published *de Vinis*, the tide of religious sentiment swayed toward conservatism and fundamentalism. Under Pope Clement V (1264–1314), the seat of the Roman Catholic Church was moved from Italy to France. The powerful Knights Templar were abolished for political reasons. A Franco-Mongol alliance was established in hopes of crushing the Islamic empire's hold on southwestern Europe. All forms of non-Christian thought were deemed as heresy. Thus, de Ville-Neuve's collected works were not published until 1504. But three of his contemporaries spread the word about *aqua vitae*, even before his death.

Ramon Lull

D OCTOR ILLUMINATUS reputedly learned distillation from de Ville-Neuve himself. Born in Mallorca, Ramon Llull (1232–1315) was a well-educated nobleman who tutored James II of Aragon before he had a religious epiphany and became a hermit from 1265 until 1274. Returning to life among humankind, Llull entered the Franciscan order where he was highly regarded for his linguistic abilities in Latin, Catalan, Occitan, and Arabic.

In 1297, Llull was invited by King Edward II to visit Britain, where he demonstrated some of his findings in distillation and in early computation. This trip led to meetings with the Oxford theologian and logician Duns Scotus, who gave Llull his nickname Doctor Illuminatus. (Scotus himself went by the moniker Doctor Subtilis.)

Amid Llull's more than 260 works, there is one word he coined from Arabic that is still used today: alcohol.

Unfortunately, Llull also suffered for his forward thinking. He was vocally opposed for his radical views on rational mysticism by Grand Inquisitor Nicolau Aymerich, which naturally led to his exile from Spain. In his quest to convert

Muslims to Christianity, Llull journeyed to Algeria in 1314, where an angry Muslim crowd attacked and wounded him. He was carried back to Majorca, where he died.

Amid Llull's more than 260 works, there is one word he coined from Arabic that is still used today: alcohol. And he wrote one passage that most eloquently defined it. In his book *Secunda Magia Naturalis*, he commented that it was "an element newly revealed to man, but hid from antiquity because the human race was then too young to need this beverage which was destined to revive the energies of modern decrepitude."

Roger Bacon

ANOTHER Franciscan friar Roger Bacon (1214–1294) was enlightened after translating al-Razi's *Kitab Sirr al-Asrar* ("Secret of Secrets") and publishing it in Latin as *Secretum Secretoum* in the 1250s. An Oxford don, Bacon taught for a time at Le Sorbonne. There, he probably encountered de Ville-Neuve, who also lectured there. There is also no doubt that Bacon knew Duns Scotus, dubbed him Doctor Mirabilis.

When Bacon entered the Franciscan order around 1256, he was restricted from publishing his studies and was banned from teaching. But his friend Pope Clement IV did give him per-

Roger Bacon spread the word aout alcohol to the British Isles.

mission to write his *Opus Magus* and a few alchemical and astrological works over the next decade.

Like his contemporaries, Bacon fell afoul of the Church. In the late 1270s, he was placed under house arrest by the order's head Jerome of Ascoli because of his studies of taboo topics. Returned to Oxford, around 1278, Bacon continued his work without communication with the outside world until his death. It is Bacon's translation of al-Razi's work that contributed to the dissemination of distilling knowledge throughout the British Isles.

Albertus Magnus

AGAINST his family's wishes, German alchemist Albertus Magnus (1206–1280) entered the Dominican order around 1223 and studied in Bologna before becoming a lecturer at the University of Cologne. In 1245, he accepted a position at Le Sorbonne, where he no doubt encountered de Ville-Neuve, Llull, and possibly even Bacon.

This is it: Our Water of Life, Vinegar of the Philosophers, Virgin's Milk which reduces the bodies to their first matter.

Nicknamed Doctor Universalis, Magnus's study of distillation led to the publication of the book *Compositum de composites*, in which he described the process: "Leave it to ferment, the impurities drop to the bottom and the water passes from yellow to red. At this time, you will retrieve the flask and you will put it over the cinders of a very mild fire. Adapt to it the head of the alembic with a recipient. Begin the distillation slowly. That which passes, bit by bit, is our Water of Life. … Continue the fire gently until all the water of life has distilled gradually over. Then, stop the fire, let the furnace cool and conserve with care your distilled water. This is it: Our Water of Life, Vinegar of the Philosophers, Virgin's Milk which reduces the bodies to their first matter, It was given an infinity of names."

Ordained as a bishop by Pope Alexander IV in 1260, Magnus returned home to Germany. However, unlike his colleagues, Magnus was beatified and later canonized a Catholic saint. His writings introduced Germany and Eastern Europe to distillation.

O F COURSE, these four men weren't the only ones reading all this alchemical literature and experimenting with variations of *aqua vitae*. As we mentioned before, the Moors in Spain were producing *aqua vini* by then. But someone in Ireland must have gotten hold of a copy of de Ville-Neuve's *Liber de Vinis* and possibly corresponded with Roger Bacon. Because by 1320, the following passage appeared Bishop Richard Ledred's *Red Book of Ossory*:

"Simple aqua vitae is to be made in the following manner: take choice one year old wine, and rather of a red than of a thick sort, strong and not sweet, and place it in a pot, closing the mouth well with a clepsydra made of wood, and having a linen cloth rolled round it; out of which pot there is to issue a cavalis leading to another vessel having a worm. This latter vessel is to be kept filled with cold water, frequently renewed when it grows warm and the water foams through the cavalis. The pot with the wine having been placed previously on the fire, distil it with a slow fire until you have from it one half of the quantity of wine that you put in."

The Irish called "the water of life" by its Gaelic name *uisce-beatha*, which eventually became the word "whiskey."

The Crusaders & the Merchants

∞

AFTER THE FIRST CRUSADE in 1095, Genoese merchants, trading with the Near and Middle East, imported arrack along with spices and silks. (For further information on the role Genoese and Venetian merchants played in introducing Europe to distilled spirits, see Chapter 2.) Naturally, Crusaders returning from subsequent campaigns had a taste for Asian goods when they got home, helping to make Genoa and Venice two of Europe's most powerful merchant cities by the Fourteenth Century.

Although Genoese ambassadors en route to Lithuania presented Russian Grand Prince Dmitri Ivanovich Donskoi with a bottle of arrack in appreciation for his kind hospitality in 1386, the spirit did not move him. He and his court preferred beer and mead to distilled alcohol. It did, however, strike chord with the next prince. Another group of emissaries presented Grand Prince Vasily the Second Vasilievitch and his court with a bottle in 1429. Within a few years, monasteries were ordered to produce a grain-based version called bread wine. [14] In Poland, grain-based *aqua vitae* appeared in the Sandomirez Court Registry in 1405. And Genoese trading post in the Crimean city of Caffa introduced the spirit in the Ukraine around the same time.

In the meantime, in France, commercial production of armagnac had begun by 1411, becoming a registered commercial product in 1414 in Saint-Sever in Landes. The Dutch picked up on this and began production of a spirit themselves, calling it *brandewijn* ("burnt wine").

Genoa's traders gradually abandoned their lucrative Asian trade. (Their unintentional importation of the Black Plague to most of central and western Europe likely influenced their decision.) In 1381, their attentions turned toward northern Europe. Besides Russia, they introduced England to arrack in 1430, marketed as *aqua vitae*, which the

14   Zabtlinny, M. *The Russian People: Their Habits, Rites, Traditions, Superstitions, and Poetry* (Moscow, 1880).

Genoese had begun to produce in Italy.[15] It's no wonder that a few decades later an English edition of de Ville-Neuve's *Liber de Vinis*, published in 1478, was a bestseller as were the works of Roger Bacon and Albertus Magnus, thanks to a new device invented by Johannes Gutenberg—the printing press.

Not to be left behind, the Germans started distilling kirschwasser from black cherries. It became so popular by 1493, one physician in Nuremberg cautioned: "In view of the fact that everyone at present has got into the habit of drinking *aqua vitae* it is necessary to remember the quantity that one can permit oneself to drink and learn to drink it according to one's capacities, if one wishes to behave like a gentleman."[16]

Back in the British Isles, word flowed from both England and Ireland to Scotland about *aqua vitae*, where its was also called *uisge-beatha* (whisky). The spirit must have become a hot item, because in 1494, an entry in the Exchequer Rolls listed: "To Friar John Cor, by order of the King [James IV], to make *aqua vitae* VIII bolls of malt."[17] Four years later, the Lord High Treasurer's Account recorded payment: "To the barbour that brocht *aqua vitae* to the King in Dundee." Since barbers served as physicians and consequently pharmacologists as well as hair trimmers, it stands to reason distilling

15   Dorchester, Daniel. *The Liquor Problem in All Ages* (New York: Phillips and Hunt, 1884).

16   Braudel, Fernand. *The Structures of Everyday Life* (New York: Harper and Row, 1981).

17   Exchequer Rolls 1494-95, Vol. X, p. 487.

secrets would have passed from the monastery to the barbershop. By 1505, a monopoly was granted in Edinburgh to the newly chartered Guild of Surgeons and Barbers to produce *aqua vitae*.

Founts of written knowledge about distillation and just about every other subject because they knew Arabic, Greek, Hebrew, and Latin, European monasteries took a small step to join in the lucrative trade they helped to establish. Many orders initiated commercial production of their herbal *eaux-de-vie*. Benedictine monk Dom Bernardo Vincelli created one at the Abbey of Fecamp in 1510.[18] When Catherine de Medici married King Henry II of France, she brought with her cooks to make her favorite delicacies from her native Tuscany and bottles of Liquore Mediceo, Fraticello, and Elixir Stomatico di Lunga Vita, all made by monks in the mountains surrounding Florence.

The Dutch were world-class distillers by 1500. Books on the subject such as Hieronymous Brunschwig's *Liber de arte distillandi; Das buch der rechten kunst zu distillieren* (Strassbourg, 1500) clearly illustrate that the Arabian art of distillation had taken hold in the Low Countries.

18   See Hannum and Blumberg's *Brandies and Liqueurs of the World* (Garden City, NY: Doubleday, 1976) p 163 and well as Turner and Berry's *The Winemaker's Companion* (London: Mills and Boon , 1975) p 13.

T HERE YOU HAVE IT. Within a couple of centuries, the distillation of sprits in Europe went from the hottest chemical discovery to breakthrough pharmaceutical find to the coolest trend beverage amongst the nobility and the clergy.

These early decades of the 1500s also saw the birth of the New World spirits: mescal, cachaça, and pisco. Not the result of accident, these libations were born from massive shifts in Europe's political and economic arenas as the next chapter will explain.

The New World

BRASIL'S DISCOVERY AND CACHAÇA'S BIRTH

THE STORY of the New World's discovery, conquest, and colonisation is also the story of the birth of four major spirit categories: mescal, cachaça, pisco, and rum. It is a wholly unique history, just like the one we just told you about alcohol's long journey from Asia to Europe. But while Old World spirits such as whisky, vodka, and *eaux-de-vie* generally trace their heritage to the medical, religious, and alchemical trade of knowledge, these New World spirits trace their beginnings to wars, imperialism, economics, and the burning desire to conquer the wealth of the Orient, India, and everything in between.

The story begins back in Europe.

The Expansion of Trade between Asia & Europe

IT ALL STARTED with the Crusades (1095–1291)—a series of Vatican-sanctioned military conflicts aimed at saving the holy city of Jerusalem from Muslim rule—which stimulated interest in Asia's wealth of silks, spices, and opiates. These treasures were valued beyond measure amongst the European royal courts: so much so that major trade contracts established between Venetian and Genoese merchants and Asian ports were established before the end of the Crusades to maintain the flow of exotic items to an affluent clientele of nobles and later to a rising merchant class.

The writings of two early Christian missionaries helped stimulate the initial interest in establishing commerce with Asia. As historian William Stevenson remarked in his 1824 book *Robert Kerr's General History and Collection of Voyages and Travels*, Volume 18:

> "In the years 1245, 1246, the pope [Innocent IV] sent ambassadors to the Tartar and Mogul khans: of these [John de Plano] Carpini has given us the most detailed account of his embassy, and of the route which he followed. ...Besides the information derived from his own observations, he inserts in his narrative all he had collected; so that he may be regarded

as the first traveller who brought to the knowledge
of western Europe these parts of Asia; but though
his travels are important to geography, they throw
little light on the commerce of these countries.

"[William de] Rubruquis was sent, about this time,
by the king of France [Louis IX] to the Mogul
emperor:.... He is the first traveller who mentions koumis [spirit fermented or distilled from mare's milk]
and arrack..."

Reports such as these inspired numerous European merchants to travel the Silk
Route, including Maffeo and Niccolò Polo.
They moved from Venice to Constaninople in
1251; then to the Crimea in 1259; and then to
Khanbaliz (Beijing) in 1266, where they cut
out the middlemen and established direct relations
with the sources of these treasures.

He is the first
traveller who
mentions
koumis and
arrack.

Marco Polo & Arrack

IN HIS BOOK, *Il Milione* (literally translated means "The Millions" and later
titled *The Travels of Marco Polo*),
Nicolo Polo's son Marco (1254–1324) narrated how
the great Mongol emperor Kublai Khan officially
received the Polos and sent them back with Mongol ambassador Koeketei to deliver the Khan's letter to Pope Clement IV, requesting one hundred
educated people to teach Christianity and Western
customs to his people and to deliver oil from the
lamp of the Holy Sepulchre in Jerusalem. The let-

ter also contained a *paiza*, a twelve-by-three inch golden tablet that authorized the bearer to require and obtain lodging, horses and food throughout the Khan's dominion. Koeketei only traveled half way, leaving them to travel alone to Acre and then Jerusalem.

By the time the Polos returned to Venice in 1268, political commotion retarded their delivery of the Khan's letter. Pope Clement IV had died and conflicts between the French and Italian cardinals delayed the election of a new pontiff.

This was quickly followed, in 1270, by the Eighth Crusade. Led by Louis IX of France, this North African conflict caused a number of upheavals: Louis died during the campaign in Tunis, triggering a dispute back home amongst his brother Charles of Anjou, King Hugh III, the Knights Templar, and the Venetians. Asked by the Papal Legate Cardinal Ottobono to join Louis in this endeavour, Edward, Prince of England, had gone into debt to unite forces with the French king and advance into Acre, Israel.

Wth Louis's death, Edward had no choice but to continue on to the Ninth Crusade at Acre in 1271. Among those who rode with Edward from Tunis to Acre was Theobald Visconti. That same year, much to his own surprise, Visconti was elected pontiff and crowned Pope Gregory X. (The next year, the Ninth Crusade came to an end when King Henry III of England died, and Prince Edward returned home to take the throne.)

When Pope Gregory X ascended the throne in 1271, one of his first functions was to receive the Polos and the letter from Kublai Khan. It took three years to organize a journey that included the Polos—accompanied by seventeen-year-old Marco—plus two Dominican monks, who delivered the requested gift of oil from the Holy Sepulchre.

A gifted storyteller, young Marco was made a court favourite and given many diplomatic jobs during the seventeen years the family lived in China. According to Marco, the Khan was so amused by the Polos he would not give them leave to depart until 1291, when Marco was asked to escort Princess Koekecin[19] to her fiancée Ilkhan Arghun.

The Polos' arrival at the court of Kublai Khan was depicted in tapestries and books including a Book of Marvels published in France in the early Fifteenth Century.

The Polos traveled by sea for two years from Quanzhou through Sumatra, Sri Lanka, and India to the Ilkhanate (today's Iran, Iraq, Afghanistan, Turkmenistan, Armenia, Azerbijan, Georgia, Turkey, and west Pakistan). In the second volume of *Il Milione*, Marco described the trading ports of Samara, Dagroian, and Basman (Samalanga, Pidie, and Peusangan which were located at the northern tip of Sumatra in the Aceh region that he visited during this return voyage. At one point he wrote:

---

19   Marco Polo referred to Princess Koekecin as Princess Cocacin in his book *Il Millione*.

"The people [of Samara] have no wheat, but live
on rice. Nor have they any wine except such as I
shall now describe.

"You must know that they derive it from a certain
kind of tree that they have. When they want wine
they cut a branch of this, and attach a great pot to
the stem of the tree at the place where the branch
was cut; in a day and a night they will find the
pot filled. This wine is an excellent drink, and is got
both white and red. It is of such surpassing virtue
that it cures dropsy and tisick and spleen. The trees
resemble small date palms; . . . and when cutting a
branch no longer gives a flow of wine, they water
the root of the tree, and before long the branches
again begin to give out wine as before."[20]

Distillation had been introduced to Indonesia by the Chinese thousands of years ago. And this
particular region of Indonesia is still famed for its
Batavia Arrack, a distillation of sugar cane juice and
fermented red rice (aka: weedy rice) collected from
a pot still. But it appears by his description that this
was a type of arrack made from sugar palm juice that
was particular to Samara.

In the annotated translations of Polo's work
published by Henry Yule, in 1903, and Henri Cordier,
in 1920, it is noted that:

---

20   The translated text of *The Travels of Marco Polo*, volume
2 including the unabridged third edition (1903) of Henry Yule's
annotated translation, as revised by Henri Cordier; together with
Cordier's later volume of notes and addenda (1920) can be found
online at Project Gutenberg.

"The tree here intended, and which gives the chief supply of toddy and sugar in the Malay Islands, is the Areng Saccharifera (from the Javanese name), called by the Malays Gomuti, and by the Portuguese Saguer. It has some resemblance to the date-palm, to which Polo compares it, but it is a much coarser and wilder-looking tree, with a general raggedness, "incompta et adspectu tristis," as Rumphius describes it. It is notable for the number of plants that find a footing in the joints of its stem. On one tree in Java I have counted thirteen species of such parasites, nearly all ferns.."[21]

D ID POLO'S passage provide inspiration to European colonists settling in the New World? There's a good possibility it did.

Dictated to a fellow prisoner Rustichello of Pisa while he was imprisoned, in 1298, for his involvement in a military conflict between Venice and Genoa, Polo's *Il Milione*, was a massive bestseller in Europe during the 1300s and 1400s, translated into numerous European languages even before the invention of the printing press. Coupled with the popularity of arrack imported by Genoese merchants to all the European courts royal during

21   The translated text of *The Travels of Marco Polo*, volume 2 including the unabridged third edition (1903) of Henry Yule's annotated translation, as revised by Henri Cordier; together with Cordier's later volume of notes and addenda (1920) can be found online at Project Gutenberg.

that same period, New World colonists were well aware of the values of sugar cane distillates.

The fact is, the Portuguese, Spanish, French, and English were already jealous of the huge profits made by Venetian and Genoese merchants who had capitalized on the opening of Asian trade routes and their monopoly on spices, silks, and Batavia Arrack.

The time was ripe for capitalization and conquest of the entire world.

The Discovery of Brasil

THE FOURTEENTH CENTURY was a period when economic competition and national imperialism were priorities in the hearts and minds of every European ruler. No one wanted to lose a share in the material bounty that lay just within reach in Asia and Africa. Ships were built, navigators trained, and sea voyages were heavily funded in hopes of finding alternate water routes to India and China. To gain approval of their actions, these Christian monarchs sought papal benediction for their plans, citing this as an opportunity to spread Christianity to the far corners of the known world and stem the growth of Muslim influence.

No monarch was more successful at casting his net into the uncharted seas than Portugal's

Prince Henry o Navegador (1394-1460). It has been documented that Polo's *Il Milione* was the prince's favourite book. And records show that much of the information narrated by Polo aided in the drawing of the Catalan Map of the World in 1375, which Henry often referred to as his interest in exploration rapidly developed.

Founder of Europe's first school of navigation, Henry helped educate and sponsor explorers who sailed south from Gibraltar, down the coast of Mauretania, then to the Azores in 1427, and finally Cabo Verde in Senegal by 1444. At each landfall, Portuguese explorers established trade and built settlements on land leased from local African rulers.

By the time Henry died in 1460, Portugal claimed the Cape Verde Islands south of the Spanish-held Canary Islands—a point further than any European had ever reached.

Inspired by the travels of Marco Polo, Portugal's Prince Henry the Navigator paved the way to world exploration in the Fifteenth Century.

To keep future peace between Spain and Portugal—two Christian kingdoms bent on conquering the known and unknown worlds as well as securing the wealth of Asia—Pope Sixtus IV issued Bull "*Aeterni regis*" in 1481, granting Portugal rights to all lands south of the Canary Islands, from both east to west. This also reinforced Spain's ownership of the Canaries themselves.

Portugal advanced its claims to territory as far south as the Gold Coast (now known as Ghana) by 1471, and then began to set its sights on finding a direct sea route to Asia via Africa's southern tip. Explorer and navigator Bartolomeo Diaz accomplished the first half of this feat in 1487, sailing south and claiming the Cape of Good Hope in the name of Portugal before he was forced to return north to avoid mutiny by his crew.

Spain leapt ahead in the race for world domination, in 1492, with the successful voyage of Genoese navigator Christopher Columbus under the Spanish flag. Another papal bull *"Inter caetera"*— this time issued by Pope Alexander VI on 4 May 1493—reset the ownership boundaries, granting Spain all lands west and south of a pole-to-pole line positioned one hundred leagues from the Cape Verde Islands. This demarcation was much looser than a specific point of measurement, an island in the cluster, or a degree of longitude.

Naturally, Spain was pleased. Portugal was not. On 7 June 1494, Pope Alexander VI then drafted the Treaty of Tordesilhas, which gave Portugal carte blanche to claim any lands discovered between the Portuguese-held Cape Verde Islands and the Spanish-held islands of San Salvador in the Bahamas, Cuba, and Hispanola. Appeased by this decision, Portugal continued to focus on the conquest of an Atlantic passage to India.

IN 1500, explorer Pedro Álvares Cabral led an expedition of thirteen ships to India via the Cape of Good Hope, commissioned by King Manuel I and additionally funded by a group of Florentine merchants. A crew of 1.500 men captained by Bartolomeo Diaz, Luís Pires, Pêro Vaz de Caminha, Sancho de Tovar, Nicolau Coelho and others were mandated to establish permanent trade relations and introduce Christianity (with the aid of priests who were also onboard), using force of arms where necessary in the lands they discovered along the way. Explorer Vasco da Gama, who was the first European to sail directly from Europe to India in two years earlier, provided the charts and notes for the voyage.

Portuguese explorer Pedro Álvares Cabral accidentally discovered the "island" later to be called Brasil while seeking an Atlantic passage to India.

In his memoirs, *Memória das Armadas que de Portugal passaram à Índia,* Cabral recounted that the fleet left Lisbon on Monday, 9 March, following da Gama's course and taking care to avoid the Doldrums—now called the Intertropical Convergence Zone—off Africa's Gulf of Guinea until they reached the Cape Verde Islands on 22 March.

According to Pêro Vaz de Caminha:

"On the following night, the Monday, we discovered at dawn that Vasca de Ataíde and his ship had been lost, though there was no strong or contrary wind to account for this [He later rejoined them]. The admiral [Cabral] sought him diligently in all directions, but he did not appear again. So we continued on our way across the ocean on the Tuesday of Easter week, which was 21ˢᵗ April, we came across some signs of being near land, at some 660 or 670 leagues from the aforesaid island by the pilot's computation. ...On the following morning, Wednesday,...at the hour of vespers we sighted land, that is to say, first a very high mountain, then other lower ranges of hills to the south of it, and a plain covered with large trees. The admiral named the mountain Easter Mount and the country the Land of the True Cross."[22]

Leaving a handful of settlers on this so-called "island", Cabral resumed his voyage to India on 3 May, recrossing the Atlantic and reaching Africa's Cape of Good Hope by month's end. With only half his fleet remaining, he managed to make it to another island that was discovered by another of his captains, Diogo Dias, on 10 August, which he named Saint Lawrence after the saint of the day, later called Madagascar.

Remember, at the time, Portugal's main interest lay to the east in India and China. The discovery of another island in the unknown New World meant little to a king who needed his war debts covered and his coffers filled.

The one item that drew interest was the island's abundance of *pau-Brasil* (Brasilwood),

---

22 *Portuguese Voyages: 1498-1663: Tales from the Great Age of Discovery*, edited by C.D. Ley (London: Phoenix Press, 2000).

which was imported from Asia as a red dye in powdered form. This dye was a prized possession amongst the nobility who followed the trend for wearing deep red garments. The discovery of this same tree proliferating on the newly-claimed island was an unexpected treat. It only took a few years before a crown-granted Portuguese monopoly was established. It took no time before Portuguese ships were attacked by British pirates and French corsairs, who were hungry for this precious cargo. And it took even less time for British and French profiteers to harvest and smuggle the precious wood as contraband along the southern coast, especially in the captaincy of São Vicente.

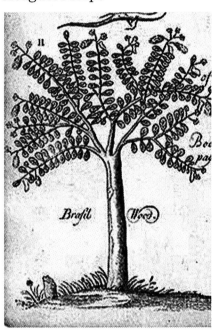

Pillage of the Brasilian forests continued unabated until the monarchy finally became interested in Brasil's colonization, thus providing extended protections for Portuguese interests in the new territory.

Used to dye garments a rich red hue that was fashionable during the Renaissance, Brasilwood was a sought-after import from Asia until lush forests were also discovered in Brasil.

In 1530, King John III of Portugal sent a fleet under the command of Martim Afonso de Sousa to ward off the pirates and to claim territory for Portugal along the meridian established by the Treaty of Tordesilhas. Among the four hundred crew and colonists on the voyage was his brother Pero Lores de Sousa who later governed the captaincies of Itamaracá, São Amrao, and Santana plus Duarte Coelho Pereira who later governed Pernambuco.

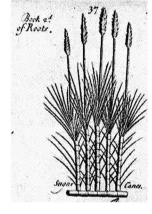
Landing on the northern coast of Bahia, de Sousa split the fleet, sending one group led by Duarte Coelho Pereira to map the northern coast, while de Sousa led the exploration and charting of the south coast to Santa Catarina. Along the way, de Sousa spoke with the handful of Europeans descended from Cabral's voyage in 1500 as well as the Tupis who had become their allies. He heard stories of the Indians in the northern interior who adorned themselves with gold and learned that the easiest way to navigate to this legendary land was up the Rio de la Plata through Spanish-held land. The hardest route was to traverse through the mountains west of what would become known as São Vicente.

Brasil's southern coast around Santa Catarina offered few natural ports or bays. But the area near the mountain passage leading to the land of gold formed a safe harbour. It was the ideal place to establish Brasil's first settlement with the legal status of village and thereby secure sovreignty. On 22 January 1532, de Sousa founded São Vicente (named after the patron saint of that given day), bringing with him seedlings of a precious crop that was being successfully cultivated throughout the Caribbean: sugar cane.

Christopher Columbus had attempted to import sugar cane seedlings from the Canary Islands to Hispaniola during his second voyage in 1493. But it us understood these died. It was definitely brought in and planted by 1503. Two years later, sugar cane cultivation was so successful in the New World that

Martim Afonso de Sousa imported sugar cane seedlings to São Vicente in 1532.

de Sousa could not resist experimenting with this valuable cash crop in the new Portuguese territory: he harvested and established one of the colony's first suceries. Duarte Coelho Pereira followed suit in the northeast in Perambuco.

With the success of this expedition, King John III established, in 1534, a series of fiefs or hereditary captaincies, similar to those established in Madeira, the Azores, and other Portuguese-held islands and lands along western Africa. Each *fidalgo* (man of noble birth) was titled captaincy general (*capitão-mor* or *capitão-donatário*) of a specific region:

REGION	CAPTAINCY GENERAL
Maranhão I	Fernão Aires
Ceará	Antônio Cardoso de Barros
Rio Grande	João de Barros and Aires de Cunha
Itamaracá, São Amaro (from Bertioga to Parati), and Santana (from Cananéia to Laguna)	Pero Lopes de Sousa
Pernambuco	Duarte Coelho Pereira
Bahia de Todos os Santos	Francisco Pereira Coutinho
Ilhéus	Jorge de Figueiredo Correla
Pôrto Seguro	Pero Campos de Tourinho
Espíritu Santo	Vasco Fernandes Coutinho
São Tomé	Pero de Góis da Silveira
São Vicente I and São Vicente II	Martim Afonso de Sousa
Maranhão II	João de Barros

In the end, only two of these original captaincies thrived in the new land: Duarte Coelho Pereira's Pernambuco and Martim Afonso de Sousa's São Vicente, where the cane plantations reputedly produced sugar of the highest quality.

The Birth
of the New World Spirits

NECESSITY HAS ALWAYS BRED invention. And the birth of the first three New World Spirits was no exception. Within thirty-five years in which the Spanish and Portuguese discovered the New World, then claimed and began to colonise it, mescal, cachaça, and pisco were born. (Rum and rhum took another century to be developed.) Their births can be traced to the prohibitive cost and difficulty of importing a regular supply of *bagaceira* (meaning "brandy") from the mother countries.

Throughout history, there has never been a significant period when humankind has not discovered, developed, and consumed fermented beverages for religious, medical, or social purposes. The New World followed that rule.

Prior to European settlement, the indigenous peoples of the Caribbean as well as Central and South America produced fermented beverages used for mainly religious purposes just as the Proto-Indo-Iranians and Hindus of India imbibed the drink of the gods, *somasara*, derived from the sacred *somalatha* plant.

In Mesoamerica, Toltec and Aztec legends narrate the birth of *pulque* or *octli*. Another gift from the gods, the beverage was fermented *agua-miel* extracted from *maguey*—the blue Weber agave or century plant—that was the most sacred plant in their religious traditions.

The Tupinambá of Brasil drank similar beverages called *cauim*, made from manioc (aka: yucca or cassava) and *avati*, made from millet. The plant was cooked and chewed by women, then re-cooked prior to fermentation to break the starch down to fermentable sugar. The method used was not dissimilar to the process employed by the Japanese in the making of the earliest-known form of sake, *kuchi-kami no sake* (which roughly means "chewing the mouth alcoholic beverage"). Jean de Léry described the process by which *cauim* was made in the 1550s in his *History of a Voyage to the Land of Brasil*:

"...These roots, aypi and maniot, serve as their chief nourishment, prepared in the way that I have described; now here is how they handle them to make their customary drink.

"After the women have cut up the roots as fine as we cut turnips for stewing, they let the pieces boil in water in great earthern vessels; when they see them getting tender and soft, they remove the pots from the fire and let them cool a little. When that

is done, several of the women, crouched around these great vessels, take from them little round pieces of softened root. First they chew them and twist them around in their mouths without swallowing them; then they take the pieces in their hands, one after the other, and put them into other earthen vessels which are already on the fire, and in which they boil the pieces again. They constantly stir this concoction with a stick until they see that it is done, and then removing it from the fire a second time without straining it, they pour it all into other bigger earthen jars, each having the capacity of about an eleven-gallon Burgundy wine-measure. After it has clarified and fermented, they cover the vessels and leave the beverage until people want to drink it, in the manner that I will, shortly describe."[23]

The Taínos (aka: Arawaks) of the Bahamas and Greater Antilles as well as the Caribs of the Lesser Antilles consumed a similar beverage fermented from manioc, called *perino* or *oüicuo* by the Caribs, or made from yams called *mobbie*.[24]

Granted, the Spanish were inspired by the Mesoamerican peoples to create what was to become known as *aguardiente de agave* or mescal around 1531. And it wasn't a stretch for the Spanish in the late 1530s to produce pisco—a grape *eau-de-vie* made in the traditional Spanish style that was

23   de Léry, Jean. *History of a Voyage to the Land of Brasil* (1577), translation and introduction by Janey Whatley (Berkeley CA: University of California Press, 1993).

24   For information on the Carib and their beverages, see "Historical Notes on Carib Territory" by William (Para) Riviere, PhD; and Frederick H. Smith's *Caribbean Rum: A Social and Economic Hisotry* (Gainesville FL: University of Florida Press, 2005).

named by sailors after the Peruvian port of Pisco where the potable was sold.

But did the indigenous Taínos and the Tupis inspire the Spanish and Portuguese, respectively, to produce rum and cachaça? Probably not. Chances are, envy of Italy's continued hold on the sugar-based arrack market was inspiration enough to establish a commodity for a market thirsty for these particular potent potables.

Although they gradually abandoned their interest in the Near East after their defeat in 1381 in the War of Chiogga against Venice, the Genoese had developed new business with Northern Europe. Making their own arrack, they continued to stimulate interest in this non-grape spirit well into the 1400s:

> But did the indigenous Taínos and the Tupis inspire the Spanish and Portuguese, respectively, to produce rum and cachaça? Probably not.

"Arrack was first introduced into England from Genoa in 1430. The Genoese, following his" (Th. de la Saussure's) "suggestion, prepared it from grain, and sold it in bottles under the name of aqua vitae, or water of life. It was so called, because from its stimulating effects it was supposed to increase life."[25]

Therefore, the Genoese merchant's influence on the European palate for arrack had more than two centuries to take hold before the births of

25   Dorchester, Daniel. *The Liquor Problem in All Ages* (New York: Phillips and Hunt, 1884).

cachaça and rum. And the first to prove this point
was Martim Afonso de Sousa.

The First Cachaça Distillery
∞

ACCORDING TO HISTORIAN Marcelo
Cámara, Martim Afonso de Sousa and
his partners Pero Lopes de Sousa,
Francisco Lobo, Vicente Gonçalves, and Erasmo
Shetz of Antwerp set up three suceries in 1533:
São Jorge dos Erasmos, Madre de Deus and São
João. They installed copper alembic stills to make
garapa azeda ("sugar cane wine") into *aguardente
de caña* ("sugar cane eau-de-vie"),[26] in 1533, just
before de Sousa set sail two tears later to accept his
post as governor of Goa, India.

Sousa sold his interests, in 1538, to Eras-
mus Shetz. The other partners followed by 1540. Of
the three suceries/distilleries they established, São
Jorge dos Erasmos remained in continuous operation until the 1700s, under the direction of the Shetz
family. For nearly two hundred years the Germany-
based family was a major exporter and distributor
of sugar, molasses, and cachaça to Europe.

Today, São Jorge dos Erasmos is regarded by
many historians and archaeologists as the birthplace
of cachaça. Since 2002, archeologists have exca-

---

26   Cámara, Marcelo. *Cachaças: Bebendo e Aprendendo* (Rio
de Janeiro: Mauad Editoria Ltde, 2006).

vated and researched the ruins of this first sucery/ distillery. It is now designated as a national monument that is open to visitors: Ruínas Engeho São Jorge dos Erasmos.[27]

The idea of colonists such as de Sousa and Shetz importing an alembic still as a basic piece of equipment is not as bizarre as one would initially think. Settling in the barbaric New World implied the need to bring essentials. A still meant medicinals including potable alcohol could easily be made. Thanks to the experiments and writings of Arnaud de Ville-Neuve, Ramon Llull, Albertus Magnus, Roger Bacon, and others, basic scientific knowledge of the distillation process was as accessible in Europe as cake-baking recipes are today. Having abundantly available sugar cane meant money could be made from not only the production of crystallised sugar, but from the distillation of potable alcohol that replicated the high-priced import Batavia arrack.

> It is now designated as a national monument that is open to visitors: Ruínas Engeho São Jorge dos Erasmos.

Obviously there was a market for this new spirit. As intensification of maritime commerce in Brasilian sugar and other products grew, and as the population increased, the number of cachaça distilleries also grew in proportion. Between 1585 and 1629, the number of distilleries in Brasil rose from

---

27 For further information on this national monument, visit http:// www.usp.br/prc/engenho/index.html.

192 to 349 operating stills.[28] (Impressive considering the first Caribbean rum distillery was not established until the 1620s in Barbados.)

Thus, rum (which according to Walter Willian Skeat was a bastardization of the Malay word "*brum*", an arrack made specifically from sugar cane, not from sugar palm like the beverage Marco Polo documented)[29] and cachaça were born and became established. These were not spirits from inspired indigenous drinks or beverages imported from slaves who were sold by greedy West African tribal chiefs, but inspired from a developed palate for Asia's Batavian arrack.

As the importation of *bagaceira*, pomace-aged brandies such as French marc, port, and other potable beverages from the motherlands cost a fortune in shipping and tax, it is not surprising that explorers and colonists who had Marco Polo as a role model were eager to produce a "local spirit" that allowed them to sustain their upper-class European lifestyle.

---

28   *Cachaça: Cultura e Prazer do Brasil* (São Paulo: Damara Editora Ltda, 2006)

29   According to the British philologist Walter William Skeat (1835-1912) the word rum is a bastardization of the Malay word "brum" or "bram,"similar to Indonesian arrack, which is also called Batavian arrack.

W HAT OF the association between sugar cane workers—who were mostly slaves and indentured indigenous people—and these new spirits at this period in time? Not as much as would happen in subsequent decades. Their drink was *cagaça,* which was a simple cane-wine substitute for the Tupis' beer-strength, manioc-based *cauim,* the Caribs' *perino,* and West African *akpeteshi* or *burukutu* (date-palm wine). None of these were distilled spirits. But the name *cagaça* does lend itself to confusion with the spirit *cachaça* and probably led to the assumption that the two were one in the same.

> Their drink was cagaça which was a simple cane-wine substitute...

This is not such a far-fetched concept as one would think. During the early days of distillation direct correlations can be found in many cultures. During the 1400s and 1500s vodka, whiskey, and *eaux-de-vie* were the rage of the royal courts of Poland, Russia, Britain, Ireland, Germany, France, and Italy. Commoners consumed beer and mead. Stills were costly machines, requiring scholarly knowledge to properly employ. Fermentation without distillation was cheap and easy. Therefore, it stands to reason that rum, cachaça, and mescal were the beverages of the colonial upper classes while *cagaça, perino, pulque, caium,* and *burukutu* were the drinks of the slaves and servants.

56

CHAPTER THREE

Mother Portugal Discovers Cachaça

A BLESSING BECOMES A CURSE
DURING THE 1600S AND 1700S

BETWEEN 1550s and 1660s, more and more Brasilian plantation owners installed both suceries and "houses for cooking honeys"—as they were registered back in Portugal by their *fidalgo*-owners. Not surprisingly, around this same time more and more high-born Brasilian settlers discovered cachaça.

The Portuguese poet Francisco Sá de Miranda (1481-1558) was an early fan of cachaça. The brother of Mem de Sá (Brasil's third governor-general, from

1557 to 1572) and a friend to King John III and the royal court, Sá de Miranda was well-regarded throughout Europe for introducing the sonnet, the elegy, and the ecologue as poetic forms to the Portuguese language. He was also known for his letters which were completely written verse. Living on the Quinta da Tapada estate owned by Antônio Pereira, the poet wrote in a letter to his landlord after first sampling a cask of cachaça (probably a gift from his brother):

Ali, não mordia a graça,
Eram iguais os juizes,
Não vinha nada da praça,
Ali, da vossa cachaça!
Ali, das vossas perdizes![30]

Translation:
There, it did not bite to grace,
They were equal the judges
Comes nothing of the plaza,
There, of your cachaça!
There, of your partridges!

This is one of the first documented uses of the word "cachaça." Before then, the spirit was commonly referred to as grappa, *aguardente* (meaning "burning water"), or *bagaceira* ("brandy").

Not only did cachaça serve as a pleasant curiosity to Portuguese nobility such as Sá de Miranda, it became hard currency for the purchase of essen-

30   *Cachaça: Cultura e Prazer do Brasil* (São Paulo: Damara Editora Ltda, 2006)

tial commodities including slaves, just as rum did a few decades later. Spirits were cheaper to produce than sugar and easier to transport. The West African chiefs who ruled the slave trade were happy to exchange human cargo for this powerful replacement for their date-palm wine. In Africa, cachaça became known as *jeritiba*.

The slaves themselves were given a ration of cachaça per day in Brasil the same way they were given rum in the Caribbean. Despite what some historians imply, it wasn't that the plantation owners wanted to keep their slaves inebriated and therefore easier to manage.

...it was not uncommon for rich men, poor men, even slaves and indentured servants, aged from infancy to death, to consume more than two gallons of alcoholic beverages per day...

During this particular period in humankind's existence, it was not uncommon for rich men, poor men, even slaves and indentured servants, aged from infancy to death, to consume more than two gallons of alcoholic beverages per day, whether it be in the form of beer, wine, or alcohol mixed with water. Beer and wine spoiled easily, making them a very fleeting refreshment at a time when water was often dangerous to drink on its own. Spirits were far less perishable and took up less storage space in the long term. Water-born pathogens such as cholera, giardia, and dysentery were responsible for more deaths than any other cause in the days before hygiene, sewage management, water filtration became commonplace. So few people drank plain water. Spirits such as cachaça, brandy, rum, gin, and the like were not only cheap to produce, they did not spoil. And a small amount of distilled spirit is sufficient to render a glass of water free of most pathogens.

There are some solid examples to demonstrate this in the annals of both European and North American history. The Pilgrims brought brandy with them when they landed at what was to become Plymouth in the New World in 1620. In fact, they sailed with more alcoholic beverages on board than water. It has been estimated that the average American colonist over the age of fifteen consumed over six gallons of absolute alcohol per year, adding up beer, wine, and distilled spirits.

During the 1600s, the average European residing in either the Old or New World imbibed brandy or rum as a eye-opener (possibly a carryover over from the Scottish Highlander's dram of whisky tradition). For breakfast, they had a bit of rum with bacon or bread soaked in beer. At 11 AM, everyone stopped work for an "eleven o'clock bitters".[31]

Around noontime, dinner was served at the local tavern offered up with popular "small drinks," many of them recognizable as British and French mixed concoctions dating back to Medieval and Elizabethan times: Bumboo, Calibogus, Cherry Bounce, Ebulum, Manathan, Meridian, Mimbo, Rattle-Skull, Rum Flip, Sangaree, Stonewall, Switchel, Syllabub, and Whistle-Belly Vengeance, and Yard-of-Flannel

31　Earle, Alice Morse. *Stage Coach and Tavern Days* (New York: Macmillan, 1900).

were just a few of the daily quaffs that passed the lips of the average person along with a half pint of liquor diluted with water that was considered part of the daily wage on land and on sea. At the end of the day, a nightcap was served up to warm the blood prior to sleep.

In the same vein, cachaça was documented in playing a vital role in Brasilian health well into the 1700s. Dr Francisco da Fonseca Henríquez wrote, in 1721, that cachaça should be sipped in the morning on an empty stomach to assure good health.[32] In the same text, he added that the spirit was "very helpful in cold and humid climates, for obese people, for the elderly, and for weak-stomached people." Throughout Brasil, cachaça was combined with herbs and spices in the making of medicinal elixirs, balms, syrups, tinctures, and ointments.

This tradition continued throughout the European sphere from the motherlands to colonized Asia, Africa, the Americas, and Australia until well into the early 1800s with one exception. The British Royal Navy, the largest procurer of Caribbean rum beginning in 1655, continued to issue its regular seamen a daily ration of two gills (a half pint) of rum per day until 30 July 1970. This had replaced a gallon per day ration of beer or quart of wine issued prior to 1655.[33] (Officers were rationed portions of gin.)

32   da Fonseca Henríquez, Francisco. *Âncora medicinal: para conservar a vida com saúde*, 1721.

33   The American navy ended its rum ration 1 September 1862.

El Draque

ANOTHER SEA-WORTHY note from this period is the invention of the mojito's precursor. Sir Francis Drake's (1540-1596) was a famed British explorer and privateer who was nicknamed El Draque ("the Dragon") by the Spanish and Portuguese because of his raids on their New World ports. Legend tells us that pirate Richard Drake invented the drink which he named after his boss. The basic concoction included readily available ingredients: sugar, key limes, spirit, and a variety of local mint (mentha nemorosa, commonly called Cuban mint or large apple mint and known locally as *hierba buena)* which grew naturally in the sugar cane fields.

Legend has it that the mojito's precursor, the El Draque, was invented by pirate Richard Drake to honor his captain Sir Francis Drake.

How did this Drake divine such a concoction? Among Francis Drake's crew were escaped slaves known as *cimarrones* who not only knew of cachaça but the locations of the northern Brasilian distilleries which the fleet certainly encountered as they scoured the coast and the Caribbean. Although many claim the drink was made with rum, cachaça was the original feature ingredient. Rum developed four decades after Drake's death in 1596.

Ramping Up Production

∞

S ÃO VICENTE was not the only large-scale cachaça producer by the Seventeenth Century. Chartered in 1621, the Dutch West India Company had a hand in boosting exportation of sugar products from Bahia and Pernambuco, especially after the Dutch captured and maintained a good portion of Brasil's northern "sugar coast" from the 1640s until 1654.

According to Portuguese registers, during the 1630s, plantations in Pernambuco exported large barrels of cachaça along with lump sugar. But in 1635, the local government in Bahia prohibited the sale of cachaça. Four years later, an initial attempt to prohibit the manufacture of cachaça was encated, leading to the burning of some stills.[34]

Concurrently, the French, Dutch, and British ramped up sugar and rum production on their Caribbean colonial islands. The price of sugar crashed with increased supply. In addition a combined French and British ban on Brasilian sugar limited its marketability.

Strained relations with Spain between 1640 and 1688 forced the Crown to depend heavily on Brasil to pay for its military efforts at home.[35] Plantation owners were imposed with high taxes on not

---

34 *Cachaça: Cultura e Prazer do Brasil* (São Paulo: Damara Editora Ltda, 2006)

35 ibid.

only sugar, but cachaça. This led to the 1660 Revolt of Cachaça in and around Rio de Janeiro. Once the rebellion was suppressed in 1661, the sale of cachaça was banned in Brasil, leaving producers no recourse but to step up shipment of the spirit to Angola. Besides the increase in exportation costs, the price of the slaves who worked the plantations went on the rise due to stiffer competition. Somehow, the suceries and distilleries of Pernambuco and São Paulo continued to thrive while operations in other regions failed before the ban was lifted in 1695.

...the sale of cachaça was banned in Brasil, leaving producers no recourse but to step up

The Gold Rush

IN THE NEARLY two hundred years that São Paulo had been inhabited by Southern Tupis, Portuguese colonists, and a handful of French corsairs, the region had enjoyed assimilation and relative independence from Portugal. Known as the Paulistas, this eclectic populace spoke Língua Geral Paulista, a dialect of Southern Tupi rather than Portuguese. In fact, most of São Paulo's population at the time was mestiço, a mix of Portuguese and Tupi. During the 1700s, their world changed with the discovery of gold and then diamonds.

The hunt for riches equal to or surpassing those found by the Spanish conquistadores in Mesoamerica had not died since Martim Afonso de Sousa first heard the tales of northern hills that abounded with gold and diamonds back in 1531. Since Brasil's discovery, expeditions called *bandeiras* were launched from São Paulo dos Campos de Pirantininga up the rivers at the edge of the Serra do Mar into the unguarded, Spanish-held interior. Led by *bandeirantes*, who were mostly Paulistas, the *bandeiras* searched for the legendary hidden cities in the Andes mountains and the mines said to be laden with gold and precious stones. (These *bandeirantes* also earned a side-living capturing runaway African and indigenous people forced into slavery.)

Despite the devastation these men wreaked on human life in the interior, *bandeirantes* such as Antônio Raposo Tavares, Bartolomeu Bueno da Silva, Fernao Dias Pais, Antonio Rodrigues Arzao, Antonio Pires de Campos, and Bartolomeu Bueno de Siqueira were also responsible for extending Portugal's claim on the nation of Brasil beyond the papal-decreed line of demarcation and in enlarging the state of São Paulo to include Mato Grosso, Goiás, Paraná, and Santa Catarina.

In 1693, Fernão Dias Paes and other *bandeirantes* found treasure closer than could ever be imagined, in the hinterlands of Minas dos Matos Gerais (meaning "mines of the general woods"), which was later shortened to Minas Gerais. Alluvial gold was found on the Rio das Velhas.[36]

When news reached Bahia and Rio de Janeiro, a gold rush ensued with thousands of fortune hunters (who the *bandeirantes* called *emboabas*) flocking to São Paulo. Between 1708-1710, the *bandeirantes* frequently clashed with the *emboabas*, leading up to the Guerra dos Emboabas (1708-1709). In the end, the Paulista *bandeirantes* were defeated.[37]

Gold prospectors working their way along the Rio Jequintinhonha triggered another rush when diamonds were discovered in 1725.[38] The boom was on once again. To stave off a mass emigration from the motherland, the Crown banned travel to Brasil.

> In Parati alone, there were over 250 distilling operations.

As mentioned earlier, despite quick success in the sugar cane market, prices had fallen during the 1600s because of stiff competition from French and British plantations in the Caribbean and northern South America. Although plantations continued to flourish in both Pernambuco and São Paulo, the largest economic boost to Brasil took place in Minas Gerais. To quench the thirst of these hordes of fortune seekers, distilleries in Parati and Minas Gerais produced an abundance of cachaça. In Parati alone, there were over 250 distilling operations.

36   See "Brasil Historical Setting" at http://www.country-studies.com/Brasil/historical-setting.html.

37   Encyclopedia of the World at http://www.bartleby.com/67/916.html#c4p03198.

38   See "Brasil Historical Setting" at http://www.country-studies.com/Brasil/historical-setting.html.

Despite the fact the *terroir* did not seem to support a thriving sugar cane crop, historian Marcelo Magalhães Godoy remarked that sugar cane, suceries, and distilleries became an integral part of the Minas Gerais landscape during the first half of the Eighteenth Century.[39]

It was during this new economic period that Portugal noticed a distinct decrease in exports to Brasil, especially of *bagaceira*. Naturally, this displeased the Crown and the royal court. A moratorium was imposed on the establishment of new Brasilian suceries and distilleries.[40] Next, high taxes were imposed on the production of cachaça on numerous levels. In 1711, the Chamber of Mariana requested royal consent to charge local suceries and distilleries a half gold coin on each barrel of cachaça and molasses produced.[41]

Brasilian governor Dom Brás Baltasar de Silveira prohibited the building of new suceries and distilleries in 1714, threatening demolition of new buildings and imposing high fines on lawbreakers.[42] During de Silveira's term, some operations were destroyed to reinforce his authority. Four years later, then-governor Dom Pedro de Almeida ordered the licensing of all sugar producers.

Nearly two decades later, Governor Gomes de Freire Andrade informed King John V that despite

---

39   *Cachaça: Cultura e Prazer do Brasil* (São Paulo: Damara Editora Ltda, 2006).

40   ibid.

41   ibid.

42   ibid.

the restrictions, the suceries and distilleries of Minas Gerais continued to proliferate. But instead of recommending suppression of these operations, the governor took another approach. In 1739, he imposed an edict prohibiting the sale of cachaça by female street sellers who hawked their wares near gold mining operations in the area. Much like the female gin sellers in London during this same period, women made up the majority of the underground liquor dealers in Brasil.[43]

However, nothing seemed to quell the flood of cachaça. So in 1743 the Crown placed another moratorium on the licensing and building of new distilleries. To reinforce this next blow, the order also prohibited the movement of stills within the estates and established distillery licensing as a royal perogative.[44]

It was noted by Jose João Teixeira Coelho, magistrate of Minas Gerais from 1768 to 1799, that none of these restrictions helped reduce the number of distillery operations. One example is Engenho Boa Vista which was established by the Chaves family in 1756 and is still in operation today. But these restrictions remained in place until in 1827, Emperor Pedro I lifted all bans.[45]

43   *Cachaça: Cultura e Prazer do Brasil* (São Paulo: Damara Editora Ltda, 2006).

44   ibid.

45   ibid.

ON THE FIRST OF NOVEMBER 1755, the Great Lisbon Earthquake triggered the near-total decimation of Portugal's largest city. The quake plus ensuing tsunami and conflagration killed approximately 90,000 of the 275,000 people who resided there and leveled eighty-five percent of its buildings. The event did as much to fan Portugal's existing political tensions as it did to end the country's imperialistic ambitions throughout the world.

Back in Brasil, a so-called voluntary contribution was imposed on the sale of cachaça to pay for the reconstruction of Lisbon. This affected not only producers. The tax was doubly imposed on suceries such as Engenho Boa Vista, who sold the spirit at retail within their estates or off premises. The tax was repeatedly renewed from 1756 until 1778.[46]

The Great Lisbon Earthquake of 1755 put an end to Portugal's push to become a world power.

An additional tax on cachaça was imposed in 1772. The Literary Tax was created to subsidise newly-arrived lay educators: replacements for the Jesuits who had been expelled from Portugal and South America in 1767, as a result of political and economic conflicts between the Crown and the Vati-

---

46 *Cachaça: Cultura e Prazer do Brasil* (São Paulo: Damara Editora Ltda, 2006).

can. The additional tax charged distilleries for each barrel of cachaça that was sold.[47]

Tax on cachaça and molasses trickled down to the mining engineers—the greatest consumers of cachça—when they were requested to pay an annual tribute for their production and purchase. (It is interesting to note that during this exact same period, the British government imposed a Sugar Tax and a Molasses Act aimed at reducing rum production in the North American colonies. It sparked a protest of "taxation without representation is tyranny" which quickly led to the American Revolution of 1776.)

a prohibition was instigated... against the consumption of cachaça based on an unfounded claim that slaves drank too much of it, got sick and became unproductive...

Next, a prohibition was instigated by the Crown against the consumption of cachaça based on an unfounded claim that slaves drank too much of it, got sick and became unproductive, thereby threatened the peace and prosperity of the colony.[48] Although the economic benefits to Portugal were as blatantly obvious as the reason for prohibiting cachaça was entirely false, this single event changed public perception of the spirit for centuries to come.

---

47   *Cachaça: Cultura e Prazer do Brasil* (São Paulo: Damara Editora Ltda, 2006).

48   ibid.

CHAPTER FOUR

The Decline of Cachaça

PROPAGANDA AND POLITICS DURING THE 1800S

A CHAIN OF EVENTS around the world changed the face of Brasil and the rest of the world during the Nineteenth Century. Between 1807 and 1808, Napoléon Bonaparte successfully invaded Portugal and Spain during his campaign to build the French Empire. This triggered the Peninsular War, which pitted Spain, Portugal, and Great Britain against France.

To safeguard the crown, Regent João, his mother Maria I (nicknamed "Maria the Mad"), and their royal court fled to Rio de Janeiro in 1808. João immediately put steps into motion to change Brasil's global status, installing a royal treasury, the Bank of Brasil, a printing office, library, university, military academy, and court of law. His royal highness's arrival also marked a major influx of higher-bred, cultured Europeans. The city's population doubled from 50,000 to 100,000 with the arrival of new Spanish, French, and British middle-class professionals, scientists, and artists.[49]

Regent João decreed the end of Portugal's commercial monopoly on Brasil. The merchants could sell to whom they chose without restrictions. This did not, however, please the merchants in either Rio de Janeiro and Lisbon. So João made some concessions. He limited free trade to Belém, São Luis, Recife, Salvador, and Rio de Janeiro. Trade among other colonial ports was reserved for Portuguese ships. The tariff on imported goods which had been twenty-four percent was reduced to sixteen percent for Portuguese imports.[50]

Great Britain further attempted to control the Brasilian market by signing the 1810 Treaty of Navigation and Commerce, which fixed a maximum tariff of fifteen percent on British textiles, hardare, and earthenware imported into Brasil. This was followed by an 18 October 1810 decree which lowered duties on Portuguese imports from sixteen to fifteen percent. But this did not to restore Portuguese trade with Brasil, which essentially collapsed. Portugal and consequently Brasil could hardly protest at the time. Britain was instrumental in helping the

49   Fausto, Boris. *A Concise History of Brasil* (Cambridge: Cambridge University Press, 1999).

50   ibid.

Crown regain its motherland from Napoleon and at the time Portuguese colonies were protected by British forces.[51]

With the signing of the 1810 Treaty of Alliance and Friendship, the Crown agreed to limit slave trade in its own territories and vaguely promised to restrict its internal slave trade. (Five years later, this culminated in the signing of another treaty that ceased all slave trade north of the equator though the fact that trade in human labour actually rose to its apex in the Americas before subsiding in the 1820s.)[52]

The new influx of middle-class Europeans and limitation of slave trade had two significant effects on cachaça production during the Nineteenth Century. A class rift between the new emigrants and the existing Brasilian population arose. Anything that was considered to be "Brasilian" was deemed lower class by the new arrivals, including cachaça consumption.

With reduction of the slave trade, the demand for cachaça—still exported as *jeritiba* to Africa—rapidly declined. Unlike rum, which enjoyed increased demand when the British Royal Navy chose the daily ration of rum as part of its seaman's compensation, cachaça did not gain British naval support despite its political ties.

The British naval blockades of sugar cane shipments to Europe during the Napoleonic Wars had

51   Fausto, Boris. *A Concise History of Brasil* (Cambridge: Cambridge University Press, 1999).

52   ibid.

triggered interest in production of sugar from sugar beets in France, further decreasing the demand for Brasil's most successful export at that time.

Despite this shift in consumer perception, reports sent to the Crown from various travelers demonstrate that in rural areas, cachaça was still very much appreciated. In 1811, an advisor to Regent João, Monsignor Pizzaro reported that the village of Januária had thirty-eight active plantations producing sugar and *aguardente de caña*. The French naturalist Auguste de Saint-Hilaire noted, in 1817, during his travels in the same area that sugar and cachaça were the first goods exchanged in trade swaps with locals.

the batida, the caiprinha's precursor, was invented by João's wife, Queen Carlota Joaquina

Some historians believe that around this time the batida, the caipirinha's precursor, was invented by João's wife, Queen Carlota Joaquina. Portuguese historian Ana Roldão discovered documents showing large monthly orders of fruits and "and average of eighty bottles of cachaça" designated for not only the queen's apartments, but those of the regent and other palace dwellers.[53] Ice was not readily available in those days, so the royal batidas were cooled on the outside of the glass with a mixture of salt and ammonia.

The royal court did not approve of João's actions, but did nothing to impede his course of expansion and improvement. In 1815, Brasil was

53   *Cachaça: Cultura e Praser do Brasil* (São Paulo: Damara Editora Ltda, 2006).

given equal standing with Portugal as part of the United Kingdom of Portugal, Brasil, and Algarves. With the death of his mother the next year, João succeeded to the Portuguese throne as King João VI.

With his enthronement, João's popularity waned in Brasil. His perceived extravagance and Europeanization of the country aroused serious opposition against absolutist rule. This was equally fueled by declarations of independence from Spanish rule by Quito (1809), Colombia (1810), Venezuela (1811), and Paraguay (1811). But unlike these neighbouring countries, Brasil only experienced one significant uprising: In 1817, a rebellion broke out in Pernambuco and was suppressed after a three-month-long military campaign.

In João's absence, British involvement in Portugal posed a threat to the Crown, especially when British Field Marshal Beresford became commander of the Portuguese army. Then the Portuguese Revolution of 1820 ensued, forcing João VI to return to home in 1821 and to leave his twenty-two-year-old son Pedro as Brasil's regent. Almost immediately, the royal court took steps to return Brasil's status to that of a colony. Fearful that Pedro might be persuaded to lead Brasil into independence, the royal court ordered him to return to Portugal to "complete his political education."

This of course provoked Pedro, who refused to adopt a subservient role. In January 1822, Pedro formed a new government with chief minister José Bonifácio de Andrada e Silva, who believed in independence under a separate monarchy. There was liberal opposition led by Gonçalves Ledo, who advocated a republican government. But minor rebellions were quickly discouraged.[54]

The next month, Pedro passed a decree stating that Portuguese laws were no longer effective in Brasil. In September of that same year, Pedro declared Brasilian independence at Iparanga and proclaimed himself emperor as Pedro I. In 1823, the British, under the command of Admiral Cochrane, helped Pedro organize a Brasilian fleet to force Portuguese troops to surrender their coastal garrisons. The United States was the first nation to recognize Brasil's independence in 1824. (The next year, Great Britain and Portugal followed suit.)[55]

Also in 1824, with Pedro's pronouncement of a new constitution, heavy taxation, and submission to European influence in Rio de Janeiro, a revolution erupted in Pernambuco which was joined by other northeastern provinces including Ceará, Río Grande do Norte, and Paraíba. It did not help matters when he closed the Constituent Assembly, stating that the body was "endangering liberty". A rewritten constitution, specifying indirect elections and four branches of government, including legislative, executive, judiciary branches as well as a "moderating" power held by Pedro himself made matters even worse.[56]

54   Mahmood, Sarwar Shafiq. "Brasil, 19th Century" which is online at the Historical Text Archive.

55   Fausto, Boris. *A Concise History of Brasil* (Cambridge: Cambridge University Press, 1999).

56   ibid.

Considered economically and administratively inefficient by the general public, Pedro stepped down on 7 April 1831. He returned to Portugal leaving his five-year-old son Pedro II de Alacantra behind as heir apparent. Brasil was governed by regents from 1831 to 1840, a time marked by numerous local scirmishes including the Male Revolt, the largest urban slave rebellion in the Americas, which took place in Bahia in 1835.[57]

On 23 July 1840, Pedro II was crowned emperor, and became the country's only native-born monarch. From that point until the rise of the republic in 1889, Brasil embarked on its second round of major evolutions.

ITT WAS DURING his reign that coffee replaced sugar as the major Brasilian export. Although the first Brasilian coffee plantation had been established in 1727 when Lieutenant Colonel Francisco de Melo Palheta smuggled seeds from French Guiana, the market for this beverage did not take off until the 1800s, when it became a popular drink amongst the European masses. The main reason for this shift was a tax on tea imports from Asia that was fifteen times higher than that of coffee in high-consumption mar-

---

57 Fausta, Boris. *A Concise History of Brasil* (Cambridge: Cambridge University Press, 1999).

kets such as Great Britain between 1810 and 1840. By the mid-1800s, the United States was the largest coffee importer, consuming more than seventy-five percent of the world's production. More than half of that came from Brasil.[58]

Because of limitations imposed by previous treaties and the initiation of the abolition of the slave trade in 1850, coffee plantations were manned by Italian and other European immigrants rather than African slaves. Before the end of the Nineteenth Century, those indentured workers bought land and built their own plantations.[59]

Pedro even ordered and drank cachaça himself...

It wasn't that Pedro II did not support the sugar industry. A great enthusiast of the new technologies that were being invented during the Industrial Revolution (which had its European and American heydays in the 1830s and 1840s), Pedro II ordered the modernization of the suceries in 1857 as well as the construction of paved roadways and a steam-engine railway.

Pedro even ordered and drank cachaça himself, like his predecessors King João VI and Queen Carlota Joaquina.

Titled the Central Mills Project, the plan was funded by British money and equipped with British machinery to improve the way Brasilian sugar was processed. Eighty-seven industrial-style plants

58   See the online article "Tobacco, Alcohol and Caffeine—Centuries of Use" at http://www.libraryindex.com/pages/2092/Alcohol-Tobacco-Caffeine-Centuries-Use-CAFFEINE.html.

59   *Cachaça: Cultura e Praser do Brasil* (São Paulo: Damara Editora Ltda, 2006).

were approved, but only twelve were built under this scheme. Only one, in the town of Campos, still exists to this day.[60]

The Central Mills Project only survived for fifteen years, because the Brasilian owners did not know how to operate the machinery or were not willing to adapt to the new technology. By the 1870s, French, Italian, and British workers in Brasil who had been operating these machines ended up buying them from their Brasilian owners. It was only a few years before European sugar beet production was stepped up and the Brasilian sugar industry hit a drop that lasted until the beginning of the Twentieth Century.[61]

It is likely that more investment would have been made in Brasilian industrialization if it hadn't been for the War of the Triple Alliance which pitted Paraguay, Argentina, Brasil, and Uruguay against each other: a struggle over the strategic River Plate region, British economic interests, and the expansionist ambitions of Paraguay's president Francisco Solano Lôpez. Although Paraguay was defeated in the end, the toll it took on Brasilian economics was severe.

Pedro's grasp on relations with the Roman Catholic Church, the army, and slaveholders also deteriorated during the 1870s. Consequently the republican movement gained political strength amongst these dominant classes. Pedro II was over-

---

60   *Cachaça: Cultura e Praser do Brasil* (São Paulo: Damara Editora Ltda, 2006).

61   ibid.

thrown by a military coup led by General Deodoro da Fonseca on 15 November 1889, and he returned with his family to Portugal.

By this time, the damage to the sugar industry and, consequently, the cachaça industry was done. Sugar was no longer Brasil's leading export and cachaça was deemed a peasant's drink that was below the rank of successful middle-class European emigrants who now economically ruled the country. Ironically, there had been improvements in the quality of cachaça production from the time when it was the drink of the nobles, middle, working and slave classes. But no one would know of this evoluton for decades to come.

> cachaça was deemed a peasant's drink that was below the rank of successful middle-class European emigrants

Still, reports of cachaça reached other parts of the world. British adventurer James W. Wells noted in his 1886 book *Three Thousand Miles Through Brasil*: "Like most roadside vendas, this had the usual store of beer, always sold as English beer; but often the only Anglican materials about it are the bottles. In this case the orthodox green metallic capsules were absent, the corks were simply tied on with string. The labels showed the red pyramidal trademark of Bass, and the names of well-known bottlers; but the beer is national and nasty, although three shillings is asked for it. The native cachaça toned down with lemon, water, and sugar is far cheaper, pleasanter, more wholesome, and refreshing."

CHAPTER FIVE

Brasil Rediscovers Its Heart & Spirit

A MULTI-CULTURAL REAWAKENING RETURNS
BRASIL TO ITS ROOTS DURING THE 1900S

THE BIRTH OF BRASIL'S modern republic, in 1889, did not heal the widening gap between European-born and mestiço-born Brasilians. In fact, matters only worsened as the United States of Brasil. President Manuel Deodoro da Fonseca confronted intense opposition in his newly-established congress and announced a dictatorship in 1891.

A naval revolt forced de Fonseca to stand down in favour of Vice President Floriano Peixoto.

His government lasted only two years. Civilian rule was put into place soon after and order was partially restored.

When Manuel Ferraz de Campos Salles was elected in 1898, his first action was to restore the nation's faltering economy. He secured a large foreign loan that was used to expand trade and industry. The initiative seemed to succeed at first as demand for Brasilian coffee and rubber from the United States steadily increased. (A recent invention, the automobile, caused the demand for rubber to skyrocket at this time.) It only lasted a few years. Then the market price radically dropped on both commodities between 1906 and 1910, sending Brasil's economy into another tailspin.

...the village's 135 plantations produced "352,930 liters of aguardente and 800,000 bricks of dry molasses"

Social and political unrest once again quaked the nation's infrastructure until the outbreak of the First World War in 1914. The depletion of coffee, rubber, and sugar sources in foreign markets drove prices and production sky high for another eight years, especially in São Paulo where Italian and German immigrants joined in investment and diversification of these industries.

In 1916, producers in Januária stepped up production of both cachaça and molasses. It was reported in the *1918 Annual of Minas Gerais* that the village's 135 plantations produced "352,930 liters of *aguardente* [*de caña*] and 800,000 bricks of dry molasses." One year later, those producers exported 450,000 liters of cachaça.

Demand for cachaça skyrocketed to the point that a handful of businessmen invested in building the first cachaça bottling plant in 1926: Januária Cristil. (Before the end of the 1950s, the town of Brejo do Amparo would have twenty-eight bottling plants.)

Despite the expansion of sugar cane production in São Paulo, national government expenditures and industrial mismanagement created another economic crisis. A large-scale revolt took place, in July 1924, in areas including São Paulo, which was quelled after six months of fighting. Martial law was declared by President Artur da Silva Bernardes for the remainder of his term (1922-1924).

During the administration of his successor, President Washington Luiz Pereira de Souza, the economic crisis deepened heralding increased labour strikes and an upsurge in radicalism. Strikes were eventually outlawed in 1927 and strict measures against communist activities were set into place.

IT WAS DURING this tumultuous time that Brasilian nationalism was born amongst two diverse social classes. From the turn of the Nineteenth Century until the 1920s, Brasilian art was a faint replica of imported European classical styles, a trend repeated in many post-colonial countries ruled by European-born upper classes and populated by indigenous and non-European peasantry.

However, the manifestos of artistic movements such as Expressionism, Futurism, Surrealism, and Cubism ignited the hearts and minds of Brasilian avant-gardists such as artists Emiliano Di Cavalcanti, Anita Malfatti, and Tarsila Amaral, writer Mario de Andrade who published *Pauliceia Desvairada*, and composer Heitor Villa-Lobos. They integrated both indigenous and populist subjects into these modern schemes, creating a wholly unique art form.

The Anthropophagy Movement received its own manifesto, in May 1928, written by poet-novelist-journalist Oswaldo de Andrade: *Anthropophagite Manifesto*. Andrade applied the metaphor of indigenous anthropophagy or "ritual cannibalism" as a way to explain how foreign influences such as the European avant-gardes' attack on cultural tradition could be consumed and transformed into unique articulations that maintained the "primitiveness" of indigenous, pre-colonial Brasil.

A leading member of the Anthrpophagy Movement, Heitor Villa-Logos combined Brasilian folk music with classic European muscial elements during the 1920s.

"...We were never catechized. What we really did was Carnaval. The Indian dressed as a Senator of the Empire. Pretending to be Pitt. Or featuring in Alencar's operas full of good Portuguese feelings."[62]

Just as in the 1800s, cachaça was seen as a symbol of rebellion against the European-born ruling and middle classes. Cachaça was consumed amongst Brasil's intelligentsia and avant-garde.

Carnaval

THE RETURN to Brasilian cultural roots and the concept of cultural anthropophagy was not only felt in the salons of the avant-garde. Toward the end of the First World War, a Portuguese-imported, pre-Lent festival was consumed and transformed by the impoverished *favela* (slum) residents who lived in the hills surrounding Rio de Janeiro and Salvador de Bahia: Carnaval.

cachaça was seen as a symbol of rebellion against the European-born ruling and middle classes

Its origins lay in the Saturnalia festivities of ancient Greece, before the Roman Catholic Church modified the event into a religious feast preceeding Ash Wednesday and the start of Lent: a forty-day period of absti-

---

62   Originally published in *Revista de Antropofagia*, no.1, year 1, May 1928, São Paulo. Translated from the Portuguese by Adriano Pedrosa and Veronica Cordeiro.

nence, fasting, and personal reflection. *Carne Vale* (meaning "Farewell to the Flesh") became the last chance for people to play music, eat heartily, drink, and dance before doing extended penance for their sins.

In Portugal, this Christian feast had developed into *entrudo*: a free-for-all in which participants threw mud, water, and food at each other in the streets. More well-heeled folk attended masquerade balls, set to polkas and waltzes, like their French neighbours in Paris. The first of these balls took place in Rio in 1840, and became more elaborate as costumed revelers paraded in horse-drawn floats accompanied by military bands.

Beginning in January and lasting forty days until Ash Wednesday, this revelry adopted more and more elements of indigenous and African-Brasilian culture. The *cordões* or "strings"— parading groups of costumed musicians and dancers—first appeared in the streets in *favelas* such as Mangueira Hill. They were later called *blocos* or "blocks".

Inspired by Parisien revelers as those depicted above by Tavik Frantisek Simon in 1902, well-heeled Portuguese and Brasilians celebrated caranval by attending elaborate masquerade balls during the Nineteenth Century.

In those early days of carnaval, Rio's high society shunned the parades as vulgar manifestations of the nation's non-European roots, and especially the music that served as its backdrop: samba.

Some historians believe that the word "samba" is derived from the Angolan term *semba* (meaning an "invitation to dance"). It was also the common

name for the dance parties held by slaves and former slaves in Rio's hillside *favelas* after slavery was
abolished in 1889. The dances had roots in Congolese and Angolan circle dances, involving gyrating
hip movements or *umbigada*.[63]

Over time samba adopted touches from
Brasilian *maxixe* and *marcha*, Cuban *habanera*,
and German polka. Pixinguinha (aka: Alfredo da
Rocha Vianna Jr.) was one of the earliest samba
pioneers. But one of samba's and carnaval's most
famous popularisers was Carlos Cachaça.

Carlos Cachaça & Samba

B ORN Carlos Moreira de Castro in
1902, Carlos Cachaça's story epito-
mizes samba's heart and soul as well
as its associations with cachaça during the Twentieth Century.

The first samba composer from Rio de
Janeiro's Mangueira Hill *favela*, Cachaça was one
of the founders of Bloco dos Arengueiro—precursor to today's world-famous Estação Primeira de
Mangueira. Born of mixed African-Brasilian and Portuguese blood, Carlos was the second son of five
siblings raised in the *favela* Mangueira, where his

---

63   http://worldmusic.nationalgeographic.com/worldmusic/view/
page.basic/genre/content.genre/samba_782

father worked as a railway employee at the Estação da Mangueira. Abandoned by his father as a child, Carlos went to live with his godfather on Mangueira Hill. By the age of ten, he paraded in Cordão Guerreiros da Montanha and other *cordões*.

At the age of sixteen, three events changed the course of Carlos' life. His mother died. Then, the person who became his life-long friend and collaborator Carlota (aka: Angenor de Oliveira) moved to Mangueira. And Carlos began playing *pandeiro* in a group led by Mano Elói, one of the recording pioneers of *pontos de macumba*. When he was eighteen, Carlos frequented the *pagodes* ("jam sessions") in Mangueira and Madureira.

Carlos disliked the taste of beer. Although most musicians drank beer at these gatherings, Carlos ordered cachaça because it suited his taste. Thus he he became known as Carlos Cachaça.

Also known as O Poeta de Mangueira (or the Poet of Mangueira), Carlos wrote his first samba "Não me Deixaste Ir ao Samba em Mangueira" in the early 1920s. His fame grew as samba hit the radio waves in subsequent years with hits such as "Dawn", "Clotide", and "I Don't Want to Love Anyone", but he never made royalties from the several hundred songs he wrote and performed. He earned his living working for the railways just like his father and continued to live in Mangueira Hill with his wife Menininha. Before his death in 1997, Carlos Cachaça saw the samba and carnaval rise from the *favelas*

Along with lifelong friend and collaborator Carlota, samba pioneer Carlos Cachaça epitomized the music and the world in which it was born: the favelas of Rio de Janeiro.

to the mainstream of Brasilian life. He was publicly honored in 1995 for his role as originator of samba and pioneer of the modern carnaval; he was even paraded in the annual competition atop a Mangueira float. His *bloco* won top honors that year.

Samba schools such as Estação da Mangueira may have originated as neighbourhood fraternal groups devoted to playing and dancing, making their major cultural emergence in 1928 at the height of the Anthropophagy Movement. Today, the *escolas* are also prominent in providing community health care and educational resources for *favela* residents. Consisting of the *bateria*—a corps of hundreds of percussionists—and dancers, each *escola* spends the entire year preparing for the annual carnaval parade and enters into competition with its *enredo* or "theme samba".

What does this have to do with cachaça? Here is one of many *enredo* dedicated to cachaça:

Você pensa que Cachaça é agua
Cachaça nao é agua, nao
Cachaça vem do Alâmbique
E agua vem do Rio Beirao.

Pode me falter de tudo
Arroz, feijao, e pao
Pode me falter dinheiro
Mais o diabo de Cachaça nao

Pode me falter de tudo
Isso até, eu, acho graço
Só nao quero que me falte
Menos à daneda da Cachaça

Translation:

If you think Cachaça is water
Cachaça is not water, no
Cachaça comes from Alámbique
And water comes from Rio Beirao

You can take everything I have
Rice, black beans, and bread
You can take all my money
As long as you leave me Cachaça

You can take everything I have
But in this only do I find grace
So I don't care just what you take
As long as you leave me Cachaça

The Clash of Cultures

∞

ALTHOUGH NATIONALISM took hold in some portions of Brasil, there was one spot where a monumental culture clash occurred between the 1920s and 1940s: Fordlandia, automobile magnate Henry Ford's bid to become a rubber baron in the Brasilian rainforests.

Henry Ford never visited Brasil. But he was determined to break the British-Dutch rubber monopoly in Asia by investing in his own Brasilian plantations. After all, the seeds used to sprout the lucrative Asia plantations had been smuggled out of

In an attempt to build the American dream in the heart of Amazonia, industrial tycoon Henry Ford discovered that his cultural values could not be imposed upon Brasilians in their own land.

Brasil in 1887. Legend has it that Ford was vexed by the high price he paid for imported Asian rubber. His cohort Harvey Firestone was not impressed with the performance of Brasilian wild rubber in the making of the tires he shipped to Ford's auto plant. Firestone wanted cultivated rubber.

In 1923, the US government initiated evaluations of Brasilian, Venezuelan, and Central American rubber sources. One report, from Carl LaRue interested Ford: one plot not far from the convergence of the Tapajos and Amazon Rivers appeared to have the ideal climate and soil for rubber tree cultivation. Ford hired a Brasilian named Villares to select a proper plot and government authorities were contacted.

Brasilian government authorities were enthused by Ford's request to develop the land, hoping it would trigger another rubber boom and stimulate the country's depressed economy. In 1927, Ford was granted 2.5 million acres in Amazonia, which he purchased from Villares, who failed to mention he personally owned the land he had located for Ford to purchase. The deal included police protection and duty-free entry of all equipment and supplies. In return, Ford promised the local and national governments nine percent of the profits after twelve years.

The steamer *Lake Ormoc* towing the barge *Lake LaFarge* unloaded its first cargo on the shores of the Tapajos in December 1928, four months after it left port in Dearborn, Michigan. Motorboats, a steam shovel, tractors, a locomotive, ice-making machines, crates of food, prefabricated buildings and white-clapboard houses, a sawmill, and a powerhouse were among the items imported to establish Companiha Industrial do Brasil on Boa Vista which was rechristened "Fordlandia". Henry Ford envisioned an American oasis surrounded by verdant—albeit malaria-ridden—jungle.

The imported US and Brasilian executive staff had the added luxuries of running water in their homes and an outdoor community swimming pool. Regular Brasilian staff fetched water from spigots outside their Michigan-style bungalows and swam in a specially-designated pool. "Villa Brasileira" was outfitted to provide the 340 workers who werer on the payroll with a tailor, shops, restaurants, shoemakers, a butcher, baker, and all the comforts of American life.

The culture clash between Brasilian workers and imported executive staff from the United States grew to epic proportions during the 1920s at Fordlandia.

Before long, problems beset the place. The uneven rapidly shifting terrain eroded. Pools of stagnant water increased the malaria threat. Attempts to drain the swamps, to cover the water in kerosene, to screen the windows of homes and offices, to spray with DDT, to issue quinine to all residents only temporarily cured the growing mosquito problem. Although shoes were issued to the *seringueiros* (Brasilian rubber gatherers), their children went shoeless. Thus hookworm was rampant. The July-to-November dry season left residents stranded as the river dropped forty feet. The hot, humid temperatures proved intolerable for the middle-American managers. And then insects and disease attacked the 1.4 million cultivated rubber trees that stood in neat rows, rather than being properly scattered to protect them invading disease. There was never a rubber harvest.

In 1933, Ford swapped part of the failed plot for 704,000 acres situated a hundred miles upriver and built another operation which he named "Belterra", with only slight variations to the original Fordlandia plan.

Ford's "healthy American lifestyle", which included a 6:00 AM to 3:00 PM work schedule still did not sit well with the *seringueiros*, who were accustomed to working a few hours before dawn and then resuming work at sunset. But they did it because they got thirty-seven cents a day—double the regular wage.

The culture clash inevitably turned violent. A riot ensued when a *seringueiro* protested the self-service food line and American cuisine that caused many of them indigestion: in Brasil, food was traditionally served at the table to workers and the cuisine was more in tune with the hot climate. Amid shouts of, "I am a worker, not a waiter!" the cafeteria was demolished with machetes. The US executives jumped into boats and waited in the middle of the river until military troops arrived three days later.

When additional workers were imported from Barbados, the *seringueiros* protested that the newcomers were paid higher wages and robbed the locals of jobs. An uprising on one payday left three Barbadan workers injured. Ford agreed to discontinue the importation of workers.

For the most part, workers complied with Ford's imposed routine even when it came to the children attending school and wearing uniforms and families using American-style bathroom facilities. They enjoyed free health care at the hospital. But they ignored other perceived strictures such as attendance at the weekend square dances, sing-alongs in English, and compliance with the no liquor rule.

On paydays, boats filled with cachaça pulled up to the dock and were quickly emptied. When management stopped the boats, they headed to houses of ill-repute set up by locals who offered the workers cachaça and women.

It wasn't until former Kalamazoo sheriff Curtis Pringle, became a manager at Belterra, that labor relations eased. He deferred to local customs when it came to planning meals and entertainment. Although Ford objected to building a Catholic church (Brasil's predominant religion), Pringle immediately erected one.

Belterra produced 750 tons of latex from its disease-resistant Asian tree grafts in 1942. But that fell far below the 38,000-ton annual harvest Ford wanted for his tire plant. Other exotic woods were planted for use as trim in Ford Lincolns, but only a handful of lumber made it to the plant: Brasil had banned most hardwood exports. Belterra's other cash crops—coffee, tea, cacao, cinnamon, and ginger—never amounted to a significant income.

When the threat of German invasion during the Second World War reached Belterra, plans were drawn to establish an airfield to thwart Nazi attack. But supply ships were deterred by German subs prowling the Brasilian coast.

By 1945, Belterra and Fordlandia were both abandoned. Economical synthetic rubber had been developed during the war years, pulling the plug on the natural rubber market worldwide. Ford sold his concessions back to Brasil for $250,000, despite his $20,000,000 investment.[64]

The plantations still exist to this day, albeit in less-than-idyllic condition.

---

64   Dempsy, Mary. "Fordlandia", *Michigan History*, July/August 1994.

Industrialisation, Americanisation, & Europeanisation

WHILE HENRY FORD was discovering the challenges of Amazonia and Brasilian culture, the Brasilian government was suffering yet another series of economic depressions and political rebellions, starting with the Revolt of 1930 led by Getúlio Dornelles Vargas.

A descendant of the landed gentry, Vargas sided with the middle class and used his powers as elected president and eventually as dictator to stimulate the economy through tax breaks, lowered duties, and import quotas. He also instigated some social reforms, including women's suffrage and social security. But this did not help with the rising tide of radicalism, which came in the forms of the Communist party and the new pro-Nazi Integralista party, which was backed by the middle class.

Throughout the 1930s and 1940s, the government and Vargas seemed incapable of balancing ideological differences, the decline of key agriculture markets, class unrest, and foreign commitments without the use of totalitarian power and military might.

Despite cuts in supplies for industry in the south including São Paulo, in 1933, President Vargas granted local sugar producers—and consequently, cachaça producers—increased production quotas through Vargas' Sugar and Alcohol Institute. This organization continued until the Second World War.

In 1941, fuel and crude oil purchased by Brasil from the United States became increasingly scarce and expensive. The government determined anhydrous alcohol could be added to stretch supplies, ranging from five to twenty percent. So it ordered the sugar producers to cease cachaça distillation and to commence production of anhydrous alcohol. With the threat of German invasion looming along the northeast coast, sugar producers stepped up alcohol production, obtaining more acreage and distillation equipment.

After the war, anhydrous alcohol continued to be an economic force, threatening the re-launch of cachaça production throughout the nation. At the 1953 National Meeting of Cachaça Producers, the recently reinstated Sugar and Alcohol Institute proposed the Cachaça Defense Plan. In his closing remarks, its president Gileno Dé Carli stated that cachaça was suffering from prejudice because it was associated with the poor and particularly African-Brasilian segment of society. He believed that cachaça consumption based on that perception would endanger the integrity of the Brasilian people as a whole.

His suggestions for reform included limiting cachaça supplies for domestic consumption; price increases aimed at reducing individual consumption; the launch of a public awareness campaign about the dangers of cachaça consumption; and the formulation of a temporary cachaça monopoly. The Sugar and Alcohol Institute managed to retain fifty percent of all cachaça produced by both small and large distilleries, redistilling this product into anhydrous alcohol for the fuel industry. This allowed the producers themselves to sell the remainder at exorbitantly high prices. The money earned by the Institute was used to finance the construction of additional distilleries and transport depots.

In less then five years, the Cachaça Defense Plan achieved all its target goals: reducing production and public consumption as well as establishing quality controls and concentration of distillation sites throughout the nation. Before the end of the 1950s, the sugar production quota in São Paulo was up six-hundred percent, making the region the nation's largest producer of that commodity. This status has changed little in a half a century, with the state producing 59.9 percent of the nation's crop: about 471,170,000 tons in 2006 and growing.[65]

The Cachaça Defense Plan was abandoned, in 1959, due to legal disputes and the government's realization that the redistillation of cachaça was too costly compared to its return.

> Gileno Dé Carli stated that cachaça was suffering from prejudice because it was associated with the poor and particularly African-Brasilian segment of society.

---

65   *Cachaça: Cultura e Praser do Brasil* (São Paulo: Damara Editora Ltda, 2006).

Tropicália

∞

ALTHOUGH SUGAR AND CACHAÇA enjoyed an economic resurgence throughout the latter half of the 1900s, off-and-on totalitarianism and the assumption of a non-Brasilian political and cultural stance continued well into the 1980s, igniting artistic flames as they had from the 1920s to the rise of Tropicalia in the 1960s.

A new samba form, bossa nova, reached peak popularity among college students and young musicians in Rio de Janeiro. (However, it was not well received in other cities such as São Paulo where bossa nova was considered the music of the bourgeoisie, not of the *favela* residents.) Musicians Vinicius de Moraes, Antônio Carlos Jobim, and João Gilberto were at the forefront of this movement. The release of the 1959 film *Black Orpheus* brought the life of the Brasilian *favela* as well as the samba and bossa nova sounds of Gilberto and Jobim to international public attention and appreciation. However, its time on top of the Brasilian charts was brief: from 1958-1963. As the music traveled and was adapted by North American and European jazz musicians it lost its vibrant soul and faded, according to many Brasilian music historians. Then a military coup in 1964, sparked yet another cultural transition.

Tropicália appeared and gained prominence not only as a musical movement, but as an art form, featuring the rich imagery and sounds of African-Brasilian culture as well as the class clashes that were taking place within the nation. Artists Hélio Oiticica, Lygia Clark, Rogério Duprat and Antonio Dias were at its forefront. A new movement in film also arose: Cinema Novo. Some of the earliest examples of this new-wave cinema include Glauber Rocha's *Terra em Transe*, Joaquim Pedro de Andrade's *Macunaima*, and Rogerio Sganzerla's *Red Light Bandits*. And once again, the symbol of the true Brasilian spirit was cachaça.

The name "Tropicália" was derived from Hélio Oiticica's eponomously titled art installation and was intentionally based on the 1920s Anthropophagy Movement: assimilating influences from various domestic sources and creating something uniquely Brasilian.

On the musical side, Caetano Veloso and Gilberto Gil wrote the movement's manifesto when they recorded the 1968 album *Tropicália: ou Panis et Circenses*. Os Mutantes and others followed, driven by "socially-aware" lyrics and political activism. The next year, the movement ended when Veloso and Gil were jailed for a month for political activities and then exiled. Both relocated to London until 1972, introducing the world to their sound while preserving its Brasilian core. Artists in other media also went into self-exile—to the US and to Europe—throughout the decade and into the next.

SINCE THE EARLY 1990s and the realization of democracy in Brasil, the nation has found in itself the true meaning of its heart and spirit. There are few cities and towns where being Brasilian is not taken to heart as an identity that is unique unto itself, accepting the many ethnicities that are woven into its fabric. And rather than emulating those influences, Brasilians integrate them and reinvent them.

When you look at soccer, do you think of Brasil as a copycat of Italy or do you think of the powerful playing style of Pelé? When you listen to samba in its variegated forms, do you think of jazz or tango, or do you envision carnaval? When you think caipirinha, do you think Brasilian rum or do you think cachaça? Hopefully by now you should understand the true spirit of Brasil.

PART TWO
∞

THE ANATOMY OF CACHAÇA

The Heart of Cachaça

A BRIEF HISTORY OF SUGAR CANE

SUGAR HAS HELD its place in the hearts and on the palates of humankind for thousands of years. The word sugar itself stems from the Sanskrit *sharkara* (meaning "sugar" and also "gravel") that comes from *ikshu, ikshura*, and *ikshava* (meaning "sugar cane").[66] In the *Puranas*[67] (an oral tradition from India circa 1500 BC that was later published as a document), the Sea of Sugar

---

66   Stubbs, William C. *Cultivation of Sugar cane in Two Parts, Part First. Sugar Cane: A Treatise on Its History, Botany, and Culture* (Daniel Gugel Purse, 1901)

67   An oral tradition among Indo-Europeans that developed around 1500 BC and culminated in written texts around 500 BC, similar to the Vedas. Predecessors to the Hindus of India, these texts make up the body of knowledge of Hinduism.

OPPOSITE PAGE:
The heart of cachaça, sugar cane originated in Asia and was gradually imported to Europe and the New World.

Cane is one of the four great seas that surround the island of the mother goddess Lalita Devi.[68]

It is documented in the *Gandharva Veda* that *arka* (meaning "essence" and "liquor") was distilled from sugar cane. This word is the root of the term "arrack."

According to some authorities, this tropical grass probably originated in New Guinea in prehistoric times and spread into India, the Malayan Archipelago, and some Melanesian and Polynesian islands.[69] The process of making sugar through the evaporation of sugar cane juice by leaving it in the sun until it looked like gravel had been developed in India by 500 BC.

> It is documented in the Gandharva Veda that arka was distilled from sugar cane

This remarkable sweet was discovered by the Macedonians after the Battle of Hydaspes in 326 BC. Alexander the Great's forces had defeated the army of Raja Puru, ruler of a Punjabi state. An alliance was formed between the two leaders because Alexander

---

68 In the description of the universe given in the *Puranas*, is found the following account: The Bhu-mandala, or the planetary system of the Earth is divided into seven islands, which lie in concentric circles. The central island (of which our Earth is a part) is called Jambudvipa, the next one is Plaksha, then Shalmali, Kusha, Krauncha, Shaka and finally Pushkaradvipa forms the last and widest circle. In between every two islands there is an ocean, each of a different subtance. Jambudvipa is surrounded by Ksara-uda, or saltwater ocean, Plakshadvipa by Ikshu-rasa, or sugar cane juice, Shalmalidvipa is surrounded by Sura, or liquor, then the next is Ghrita (clarified butter), Kshira (milk), Dadhi-manda (emulsified yogurt) and Suddha-uda (sweet water). The names of these oceans are closely similar to the names of the seven Saptamshas.

69 Rosenfeld, Arthur H. *Sugar Cane Around the World* (Chicago: University of Chicago Press, 1955).

was greatly impressed by the Puru's bravery. It was during this time that Alexander's admiral of the fleet he had built at Hydaspes experienced and documented the properties of north Indian sugar cane (*Saccharum barberi Jeswiet*). He called it a "reed that gives honey without bees." Writers of the day including Paulus Egineta, Dioscorides, Pliny, and Seneca lauded the sweetness and quality of Indian sugar cane and its *sakchar* or *sakcharon*, in Greek (saccharum, in Roman).

The Kingdom of Funan in India sent sugar as a tribute to China in 286 AD. Quickly, the Chinese refined the art of cultivating a varietal cane, *S. sinese Roxb.*. The Emperor Tsai-Heng sent agents in the 600s to Bihar, India to study the art of sugar manufacture. Indian sugar cane cultivation and sugar production techniques spread during the Muslim Agricultural Revolution (700-1200 AD). *Sakkar* or *sukkar* became known throughout the Islamic Empire. From Persia, the knowledge reached Syria about 680 AD, Cyprus and Sokotra around 700 AD, and Morocco about 709 AD.[70]

Mediterranean sugar production began with the Saracen conquest of Egypt in 641 AD. Abdur-Rahman is credited with introducing sugar to Spain around 740 AD, after the Iberian Peninsula was conquered. By the time the Muslims were driven from Spain in the Twelfth Century, 75,000 acres of sugar cane were cultivated and processed in Andalucia and the Algarve alone.

---

70   Rosenfeld, Arthur H. *Sugar Cane Around the World* (Chicago: University of Chicago Press, 1955).

Portugal's Prince Henry o Navegador exported sugar cane seedlings (probably the *puri* or *pooree* varietal) to Madeira in 1420 and then to the Canary Islands, Azores, and Cape Verde Islands. By 1480, sugar cane was also being planted in West Africa. This particular variety of sugar cane was later called Creole when it was exported to the West Indies.[71]

Christopher Columbus, on his second voyage in 1493, brought sugar cane seedlings from the Canary Islands to Hispaniola. This first shipment was said to have been lost. And Pedro de Atienza is actually credited with its introduction to the Caribbean in both 1505 and 1506. The first sugar was milled there in 1509. The island had twenty-eight mills by 1518.[72]

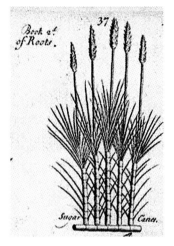

Portugal's Henry the Navigator was one of the first Europeans to export sugar cane seedlings from southern Europe along the West African coast.

According to some historians, sugar cane was brought to Brasil in 1504 or 1505 by the Portuguese, but was probably lost as it was during Columbus's voyage. Evidence does prove, however, that Martim Afonso de Sousa and Francisco Romeiro successfully imported and planted cane in that country in 1532.

Almost simultaneously, other Portuguese explorers introduced the plant to the island of St.

71 Rosenfeld, Arthur H. *Sugar Cane Around the World* (Chicago: University of Chicago Press, 1955).

72 ibid.

Thomas.[73] The German soldier and mariner Hans Staden documented the booming Brasilian sugar trade in a 1557 account of his voyage and capture by the Tupis two years earlier. In *Warhaftige Historia und beschreibung eyner Landtschafft der Wilden Nacketen, Grimmigen Menschfresser-Leuthen in der Newenwelt America gelegen* ("True Story and Description of a Country of Wild, Naked, Grim, Man-eating People in the New World, America"), he reported the existence of eight hundred suceries in Santa Catarina as well as two thousand in northern Brasil, Demerara, and Surinam.

By 1620, *puri* (aka: Creole) sugar cane had been planted and harvested throughout the Caribbean, Mexico, Brasil, Peru, and the Argentine. But a little over a century later, this "noble" cane was replaced by other varieties, including Cheribon, Preanger, and especially Bourbon.[74]

The late 1700s saw the replacement of slave labour with mechanised sugar production methods. In Jamaica, steam engines powered mills. By 1813, cane juice was no longer boiled in open kettles. Thanks to British chemist Edward Charles Howard, a closed vessel, partial-vacuum steam system

The many varieties of sguar cane were a source of fascination to botanists for centuies.

73   Rosenfeld, Arthur H. *Sugar Cane Around the World* (Chicago: University of Chicago Press, 1955).

74   ibid.

proved, in 1813, that reduced fuel consumption and reduced carmelisation of sugar were possible. In 1845, African-American engineer Norbert Rillieux developed a multi-effect evaporator that minimized heat waste. And in 1852, the centrifuge was introduced as a means for separating sugar from molasses by David Weston in Hawaii.

TODAY BRASIL continues to overshadow most countries with roughly thirty million tonnes of cane sugar produced in 2006, while India produced twenty-one million, China eleven million, and Thailand and Mexico roughly five million each. Viewed by region, Asia predominates in cane-sugar production, with large contributions from China, India and Thailand and other countries combining to account for forty percent of global production in 2006. South America comes in second place with thirty-two percent of global production; Africa and Central America each produce eight percent and Australia five percent. The United States, the Caribbean and Europe make up the remainder, with roughly three percent each.[75]

---

75 Statistics are from the Food and Agriculture Organization of the United Nations.

What Is Cachaça

A BASIC LESSON ON WHAT MAKES CACHAÇA UNIQUE

O KAY. Rum, rhum, and cachaça all begin with sugar cane. However, this simple fact does not make them one in the same. Granted, cachaça was and in some cases contniues to be imported to the United States and other countries labeled as Brasilian rum. This is because the legislation in those countries has not expanded its view of spirits to include some of the unique "ethnic" categories that exist in the world. So what are the points of difference?

First, let's look at the parallels that have caused generations of experts to group them together. All are spirits made with sugar cane`–or its derivatives. All are produced as unaged and aged products. All originated in the New World, particularly in the Caribbean and South America.

The Differences

Rum

T HE MOST ESSENTIAL difference between rum and cachaça? Rum is commonly made from molasses, a by-product from sugar refinement. Rum can be produced anywhere in the world. In fact, molasses was once imported to New England and Canada in such abundance that North America's northeastern coastline was the largest rum producing region in the world. The rum from Medford, Rhode Island was extremely prized by mixologists prior to the enactment of prohibition in the United States. Rum was also produced in the other parts of North America, including New England states, New York, New Jersey, and the Canadian Maritime Provinces as early as the mid-1600s.

But where did rum originate? Most historians believe that rum was first distilled in Barbados around 1640. The British settled the island in 1627, initially planting cotton, indigo and tobacco. But these cash crops did not yield a profit. The Dutch West Indies Company captured Pernambuco in northern Brasil by the 1630s and are generally considered responsible for introducing Barbadan plantation owners to the secrets of sugar cane growing and possibly distillation. When Pernambuco was recaptured by Brasilian forces, Dutch plantation owners such as James Holdip and James Drax brought both seedlings and knowledge with them, launching a new industry on Barbados.

Since those days, Caribbean rums are made in a variety of ways. Haitian rums use *Schizosaccharomyces* as the main yeast source. In Jamaica, dunder—the yeast-rich foam left over from the previous batch of rum fermentation—is used to start the yeast culture of the next batch.

During the 1800s rum producers in Cuba such as Bacardi developed faster working, controlled, secret-recipe yeast cultures that produce few esters during fermentation. Using a pot or column still, the rum is collected between eighty percent to ninety-four percent ABV.

Rhum

Rhum was similarly developed in French-held Martinique around 1644. According to some authorities, a Dutch-Jewish emigrant from Brasil named Benjamin Da Costa introduced sugar-making equiment and alembics to the island after Pernambuco's recapture. But it is also recorded that there was some experimentation in making *eau-de-vie de cannes* going on at least four years earlier when it was noted that the slaves were fond of "a strong *eau-de-vie* that they called *brusle ventre* [stomach burner]."[76]

The early spirit derived from fresh sugar cane juice that Martinique distillers produced was commonly called *guildive* and only later called *rhum*. The method for making the spirit known as *rhum agricole* was improved by Homere Clément in the 1800s. Fermented with common baker's yeast (*Saccharomyces cerevisiae*) to make a 4.5 percent to nine percent ABV cane wine called *vesou*, the juice is distilled in single-column stills to about seventy percent to ninety percent alcohol. This technique continues to be employed to this day.

After distillation, the spirit is aged in large vats from one to six months before it is bottled. For aged *rhum agricoles*, the spirit is matured for years in oak barrels. In November 1996, *rhum agricoles* made in Martinique using this process were given a French Appellation d'Origine Controlée (AOC) designation.

This differentiates them from *rhums* made from molasses distilled through column or continuous stills which are subsequently called *rhums industriels*: descendants of *tafia*, a distillate made from a blend of sugar scum and molasses that also appeared during the 1660s.

76 Breton, Jacques. "Relation de l'establissement des Francois depuis l'an 1635 en l'isle de la Martinique," *Généalogie et histoire de la Caribe* (December 1996).

Cachaça

By comparison to rum and *rhums*, cachaça can only be produced in Brasil as it is protected by a government designation. But that is only a minor point. Within Brasil, cachaça is only produced near sugar cane fields as it can only be made from fresh cane juice, pressed from fresh-cut plants. The cane cannot be cut more than twenty-four hours before it is pressed or it will not be useable for cachaça. Once the juice is pressed it cannot be preserved. The process must begin at once. Thus, cachaça is always made fresh from the field.

Within the cachaça category, there are differences. Similar to *rhum*, cachaças are delineated by the style of production: artisanal and industrial.

Industrial Cachaça

Made by medium-sized and large-scale mills (mostly located in the states of São Paulo and Ceará), industrial cachaça is produced in column stills, using a continuous distillation process. This allows the spirit to maintain a number of higher alcohols and esters. However, because the spirit is collected at a higher temperature, it does not achieve the distinctive character that can be crafted using pot stills which operate at a lower temperature.

Employing a continuous disllation process, industrial cachaças employ column stills that distill spirit at a high temperature as the ferment or wash continuously flows through the still.

This particular style is marketed mainly to lower economic classes at a lower price point. The exceptions to this rule are brands such as Ypióca and Sapupara, both produced by the Ypióca Group that distills and ages all of their own product on its estate. Much of this product is gathered, blended, and sold in bulk to bottlers for brands such as 51, Velho Barreiro, Tatuzinho, Pitu, 21, and Colonial.

Unfortunately for the rest of the world, these industrial cachaças also account for the bulk of exported product.

Artisanal Cachaça

Ferment or wash heated inside a pot or alemic still is distilled at lower temperatures, producing a spirit with distinctive character.

Produced throughout Brasil on thousands of large and small alembic stills, artisanal cachaças are also distilled from fresh sugar cane juice. Spontaneous fermentation in open vats is sometimes aided by the introduction of a maize-and-rice-based yeast called *fubá* or *fermento caipira*, a method popularly employed at distilleries in Minas Gerais. This is done to provide extra protein to the developing yeast culture. In the case of Sagatiba Velha, this practice is employed at the start of each production season. The spirit is collected between seventy-six percent to ninety-six percent (generally ninety-three percent) from the mids or *cachaça boa* at eighty degrees Celsius (176 degrees Fahrenheit). After distillation, some producers add up to six grams per litre of sugar before bottling.

Cachaça versus Aguardente

Although sometimes cachaça is referred to as *aguardente de caña* (meaning "burning water from cane"), it is not. Another traditional Brasilian spirit, *aguardente de caña* is collected at thirty-eight percent to fifty-four percent ABV, while cachaça is collected at thirty-eight percent to forty-eight percent ABV. Both cachaça and *aguardente* can contain up to six grams per liter additional saccharose after distillation. (*Aguardente de Caña Adoçada* or aged *aguardente* can contain from six grams per liter to thirty grams per liter additional saccharose after distillation.)

Another designation, *destilado alcoólico simples de caña-de-açúcar*, is collected at two specific points: superior (fifty-four percent ABV) and inferior (seventy percent ABV)/

Unlike cachaça, *aguardente de caña* can be also made from treacle, the final byproduct of the sugar making process.

As the ambiguity of the name implies, *aguardente* can be made from substances other than sugar. An *aguardente* can be and is sometimes made from fruit, cereal, potatoes, beetroots, ginger, vegetables, cashew fruit (called *cajuina*) a mixture of sugar cane with extracts, an infusion with spices, or manioc (*tiquira*, a descendant of *caium*).

The True Point of Difference

What really makes cachaça different? Simply put, the major points of difference among cachaça and other sugar cane spirits include the type of yeast and fermentation method; the percentile range in which the spirit is collected; the types and levels of congeners and minerals found in the spirit.

Even though the chemical profiles between the use of molasses and fresh-pressed sugar cane juice cannot be distinguished, the analysis of the SO_2 of the fermented must, the water, and even the metal content of the distillation equipment does yield features that are unique to each category.

This is not a new way of looking at this sort of question. The content of higher alcohols is used to certify Irish whiskey authenticity and differentiate Chivas Regal from other blended Scotch whiskies; the content of organic acids and esters is used to differentiate between expensive and cheap rums; and the concentrations of alcohol, esters, and fatty acids is used to differentiate the origin of wines. Metal content is also used to distinguish type, origin, and authenticity of teas, beers, and wines.[77]

One study showed that cachaça contained higher levels of propanol, iso-butanol, iso-pentanol,

---

77   Cardoso, D.R., Andrade-Sopbrinho, L.G., et al. "Comparison between Cachaça and Rum Using Pattern Recognition Methods", *Journal of Agricultural and Food Chemistry*, 2005.

and copper than rum. While rum contained higher levels of proto-catechuic acid.[78]

	CACHAÇA	RUM
Propanol	126-352 mg per liter	15.3-274 mg per liter
Iso-butanol	133-262 mg per liter	9.79-212 mg per liter
Iso-pentaol	505-774 mg per liter	3.84-347 mg per liter
Manganese	0.24-2.7 mg per liter	0.018-1.6 mg per liter
Magnesium	0.002-0.072 mg per liter	0.0020-0.069 mg per liter
Copper	0.24-5.2 mg per liter	0.015-0.22 mg per liter
Proto-catechuic acid	trace	0.100-2.66 mg per liter

Researchers at the Aguardente Chemical Development Laboratory (LDQA), of the São Carlos Chemical Institute of the University of Sao Paulo (USP) have worked diligently to determine what factors differentiate cachaça from its later relations rum and *rhum agricole*. Established some twelve years ago by Professor Douglas Wagner Franco, the laboratory seeks to chemically investi-gate cachaça. During 2004, the group collaborated, through chemical confirmation, about the differ-

Sugar cane fresh from the field is crushed and pressed to extract the juice in a grinder such as this one.

78   Cardoso, D.R., Andrade-Sopbrinho, L.G., et al. "Comparison between Cachaça and Rum Using Pattern Recognition Methods", *Journal of Agricultural and Food Chemistry*, 2005.

ences between rum and cachaça with a study group in the United States.[79]

Afterwards, the researchers continued their work to better understand the organic and mineral composition of cachaça. They have now developed methods and systems of classification that will aid in the improvement of the whole category. The researchers have developed techniques that reveal, for example, if the drink was produced in small artisanal stills or in a large distillery, if the sugar cane used was burned or not.[80]

"We also analyze the minimum quantity of components demanded by legislation and we informed the manufacturers, principally helping the small producer who plants sugar cane, harvests, ferments the juice, distills and bottles", explained Dr. Daniel Rodrigues Cardoso. Many associations and producer cooperatives are striving yo boost their quality via laboratory analyses. Within a public policy project financed by FAPESP, and without any cost to the producer, they are carrying out analyses, indicating solutions and complementing their work with lectures by group members.[81]

Legislation has substantially changed for cachaça producers in the past ten years. Limits have been imposed on mineral and chemical compounds. Recently, Canada and Germany have demanded cer-

79   "Cachaça Revealed: Studies Increase Knowledge About the Drink and Contribute to Its Quality", *Pesquisa FAPESP* (Ciência e Tecnologia no Brasil, São Paulo State Research Foundation), Issue 128.

80   ibid.

81   ibid.

tification of the presence of various components, among them ethyl carbamate,[82] methanol, and other alcohols. Because of these studies, compliance and improved production methods are now running hand in hand.

During 2005, a study of 108 cachaças collected in the state of São Paulo—Brasil's largest production region—demonstrated that seventy-five percent complied the new rulings, with levels registering below five grams per liter. In 2003, during a similar analysis, sixty percent showed compliance. Only twenty-seven of these samples were collected from large-scale producers.[83]

In relation to ethyl carbamate, during that same year, the analysis showed that fifty-one percent of the samples were below the stipulated legislation limit. Samples collected in 2005 indicate that seventy percent possess levels below the limit.[84]

The group also discovered that ethyl carbamate and benzaldehyde are most prevalent in industrial cachaças. In the artisan cachaças the variation in chemical compounds is greater. The most prevalent are: formaldehyde, 5-hydroxy-methyl-fur-

Because of these studies, compliance and improved production methods are now running hand in hand.

---

82   The use of copper potstills in the production of artisanal cachaças is the reason this element is present in some cachças.

83   "Cachaça Revealed: Studies Increase Knowledge About the Drink and Contribute to Its Quality", *Pesquisa FAPESP* (Ciência e Tecnologia no Brasil, São Paulo State Research Foundation), Issue 128.

84   ibid.

fural (5HMF'), acetic acid, and propionaldehyde. The 5HMF is found in low concentrations in industrial cachaças, and varied in artisanal spirits. High levels indicate that pieces of sugar cane had been present in the still during the distillation process.[85]

Other components not yet controlled by Brasilian legislation are also being studied such as polycyclic aromatic hydrocarbons (PAHs), which are present when sugar cane is burned before harvesting and are also found in whisky, rum and grappa. Hydrocarbon compounds such as benzo-(alpha)-pyrene and antracene are even more potentially carcinogenic than ethyl carbamate.[86]

After 136 samples using molecular analysis chromatography, researchers traced the difference between twenty-eight cachaças produced from burned sugar cane and 108 cachaças produced from unburned sugar cane. The study showed that cachaça from burned sugar cane had an average level of twenty-one micrograms per liter of PAHs: ten times higher than those made from unburned sugar cane.[87]

---

85   "Cachaça Revealed: Studies Increase Knowledge About the Drink and Contribute to Its Quality", *Pesquisa FAPESP* (Ciência e Tecnologia no Brasil, São Paulo State Research Foundation), Issue 128.

86   ibid.

87   ibid.

ONE OF THE LARGEST hurdles for exporting aged cachaças is that many types of wood used in Brasil for constructing barrels have not been approved by the United States for use in distilled spirits production. While many of these woods have unique flavor property and have been used for generations in Brasil, the must go through an extensive testing and approval process before any cachaça produced using them can be exported to the States. While some of these unique products may never be exported, there is testing taking place.

In Sao Carlos, between fifteen and twenty types of wood are being compared to the properties of oak. Armed with a multiple-stage mass spectrometer capable of verifying the structure and molecular mass of chemical compounds, the researchers are analyzing substances called polyphenols extracted from the wood by the drink. "Polyphenols such as catechin are beneficial to health", says Cardoso. They contribute to inhibiting the deposition process of fat in the arteries. Cardoso pointed towards the best option, up until now, as being the construction of barrels from the amendoim tree (*Pterogyne sp.*), a native of the Atlantic Rainforest. "It has sensorial properties (taste, aroma, color) similar to that of oak and possesses better antioxidant activity."[88]

It is believed that the polyphenol compounds are linked to the wood's cellular defense mechanisms, and their presence depends on their geographical origin and on climatic factors. Studies were carried out on woods certified and provided by the Technology Research Institute (IPT) and by the Wood Structures Laboratory of the São Carlos Engineering School (EESC) of USP. The oak (Czech, Polish, French and Scottish in origin) was provided by Strathclyde University, in Scotland. One of the woods analyzed, *canella sassafras* (*Ocotea pretiosa*), was found to contain carcinogenic compounds such as saphrol and presented pro-oxidant properties that accelerate the progress of atherosclerosis. Other Brasilian woods under study include the chestnut (*Castanea sp.*), the *ipê* (*Tabebuia chrysotricaha*), the *jatoba* (*Hymenaea courbaril*) and the laurel-canella (*Aniba parviflora*).[89]

Divisions and Sub-Divisions of Cachaça

Cachaça

The transparent, white to silver spirit that is unaged, is the cachaça that writer Rubem Braga once called: "Blood of the earth that the Brasilian brings into his own blood." Some cachaças, such

88   "Cachaça Revealed: Studies Increase Knowledge About the Drink and Contribute to Its Quality", *Pesquisa FAPESP* (Ciência e Tecnologia no Brasil, São Paulo State Research Foundation), Issue 128.

89   ibid.

as Sagatiba Pura, are rested for sixty days prior to bottling.

Cachaça Adoçada: Sweetened Cachaça

As its name implies, *cachaça adoçada* contains added sugar. According to law, sweet cachaça contains more than six grams per liter and less than thirty grams of sugar per liter. (The same law states that true cachaça can contain up to six grams per liter of saccharose introduced after the distillation process.)

Aromatised Cachaça

Although there is no legal designation for this category, there are cachaças that are aromatized after distillation. Rather than being balanced through distillation or achieving distinction from the use of different woods during the maturation process, these cachaças are infused or aromatised with fruits, herbs, spices, or other ingredients.

Cachaça Envelhecida: Aged Cachaça

Cachaça envelhecida is matured for a period of not less than one year in 700-liter wooden barrels to achieve a distinctive colour, aroma and taste. The temperature and relative humidity of the room in which aged cachaças are matured radically influence the end result of this marriage between wood and spirit. According to government regulation, the bottled product must contain at least fifty percent wood-matured spirit to be called an aged cachaça.

There are two subcategories of *cachaça envelhecida*: cachaça premium and cachaça extra premium. Cachaça premium must be aged in 700-liter wooden barrels for more than one year, while cachaça extra premium must be aged in 700-liter wooden barrels for more than three years.

Woods Used to Age Cachaça

There are dozens of indigenous woods used for ageing cachaça including *acapu, alecrim-rosa, angelica, angico, arribá, arco-de-pipa, arco-de-pipa-miúdo, aroeira, bacuri, bicuíba-canela, capicium, carvalho Brasiliero, catamuja, cedro, faveiro, gonçalo-alves, jatobá, louro-friejó, maçura, mangue-vermelho, marmeleira-di-mato, muiracatiara, mutamba, pinhopiorra, piquá, rapicium,* and *tapinhoam.*

Following are woods are that are of particular interest to producers of aged cachaças: [90]

Amburana

(*Amburana cearensis*) A cherry tree of the Fabaceae family, *amburana* is sometimes used to mature cachaça and lower the spirit's acidity while imparting a sweet aroma. Currently an endangered species of timber tree, *amburana* is native to the regions from the northeast down to São Paulo. The varietal commonly called *imburana-de-cheiro* is a neutral wood favoured by cachaça producers in the state of Minas Gerais.

---

90   Câmara, Marcelo. *Cachaças: Bebendo e aprendendo* (Rio de Janiero: Maudad Editora Ltda, 2006); *Cachaça: Cultura e Prazer do Brasil* (São Paulo: Damra Editora Ltda, 2006)

This wood is also known as *imburana, umburana, cumare, imburana-de-cheiro, amburana-do-sertao, amburana-das-caatingas, cerejeira, cereja-galega, cereja-dos-passarinhos,* and *cerejeira-da-europa.*

Amendoim

(*Pterogyne nitens*) A peanut tree of the Fabaceae family, *amendoim* wood is much prized by cachaça producers because it is a highly-prized substitute for *carvalho* (oak) wood. It is frequently used in the cachaça maturation process because it imparts very little colour to the spirit. Because *amendoim* is registered as an endangered species, harvesting and use of this wood is strictly controlled in the few places it still grows. These include for-est reserves in and around Parana, São Paulo, Rio de Janeiro, and Minas Gerais.

Angelim-araroba

Commonly found in Bahia, Rio de Janeiro, and Minas Gerais, *angelim-araroba* imparts a strong character and colour to aged cachaça. Over the cen-turies, this tree was highly prized for its yield of a substance called Goa powder which is still use as a treatment for skin diseases. *Angelim-araroba* goes by many names including *angelim-coco, pau-pin-tado, angelim-doce, urarama, angelim-do-pará, angelim-pedra, angelim-rosa, angelim-rajado, angelimpinima, angelim-de-espinho, angelim-de-folha-larga,* and *acapu.*

Bálsamo

Another member of the Fabaceae family of trees, *bálsamo* is a very aromatic wood that imparts both strong colour and a distinctive character to cachaça. This particular wood is very rarely used in the ageing process except by a handful of cachça producers in Minas Gerais. *Básalmo* is also called *cabriuca-do-campo, cabriúva, cabriúva-parda, cabrué, cabureiba, oleo-cabureiba, oleo-pardo,* and *pau-bálsamo.*

Cabreúva

(*Myrocarpus frondosus*) Also known as common sassafras, *cabreúva* is a native of northeast, southeast, and southern regions of Brasil. Regsitered as an endangered species, cabreúva is most widely used as an essential oil that is known in Brasil for its anti-inflammatory and wound healing properties.

In the cachaça ageing process, this wood provides a distinctive woodsy-floral aroma, golden hue, and strong flavour.

Carvalho

Oak trees are not native to South America. But *carvalho* (oak) wood is one of the oldest and most commonly employed in ageing cachaça. Since the 1500s, aged cachaça producers have employed oak barrels previously used to ship brandy, cognac, and wine to impart character and colour during the cachaça maturation process.

According to Professor Jorge Hoori of the Department of Sugar and Alcohol of the Luiz de Queiroz Agriculture School of the University of São Paulo, European oak barrels from Scotland and Ireland are not as good for cachaça maturation because they can only be cut from fifty-year-old trees and are used to their limit before being sold. Today, cachaça producers most commonly purchase and import American oak whiskey barrels as well as French oak Cognac and wine barrels to impart a light sweetness, pale colour, and soft character into aged cachaça.

Castanheira

(*Bertholletia excelsa H.B.K.*) Also known as the Brasilian chestnut tree, *castanheira* is a relative of the common chestnut tree that grows in abundance in northern Portugal. *Castanheira* wood most closely resembles that of *carvalho* in its properties when employed in the cachaça maturation proess. It imparts a pale colour, sweet aroma and a soft character.

Growing naturally in Pará, Amazonia, Acre, and Rondônia, this tree is also called *castanheira-do-pará*.

Eucalipto

In terms of its use as an ageing agent during the cachaça maturation process, *eucalipto* (eucalyptus) is a novelty wood, because its aroma is very distinctive. Some studies indicate *eucalipto* imparts a light sweetness, soft character, and pale hue similar to oak.

Freijo

(*Cordia trichotoma*) This Brasilian walnut tree comes from the Boraginaceae family. *Freijo* has properties similar to the *amendoim* trees mentioned earlier as well as *jequitibá*, imparting little to no colour to the aged cachaça. Freijo is also known as: *frei jorge* or *quin*.

Garapa

(*Apuleria leiocarpa Vog. Macbride*) Not to be confused with a beverage of the same name, *garapa* is a Brasilian ash tree, found growing from Rondônia to southern Bahia and from Santa Catarina to Rio Grande do Sul. *Garapa* is considered by some authorities to be one of the best native woods for the maturation of cachaça because it creates a light, colourless spirit with smooth character. *Garapa* also goes by the names *jataf-garapa, grapia, amarelinha, garapa amarela,* and *garapiapunha*.

Jequitibá

(*Cariana legalis Mart. Kuntze*) Known by the Tupis as the "giant of the forest" the *jequitibá* tree comes from the Lecythidaceae family. The wood from this tree is prized for its use in ageing cachaça because it does not impart colour. *Jequitibá* was originally found in forests ranging from Pernambuco to São Paulo. *Jequitibá* is also known as *jequitibá-vermelho, jequitibá-branco,* and *jequitibá-rosa*.

Louro

(*Cordia alliodora*) *Louro* is a member of the Lauraceae family of laurel trees that imparts a strong cinnamon aroma and taste when used in the maturation of cachaça. This particular wood, which lowers acidity and imparts a very familiar and distinctive spice to the spirit, is used most commonly by cachacça producers in Rio Grande do Norte. *Louro* is sometimes called *louro-canela* because of its close associations with cinnamon.

Palha

A pale substitute for *carvalho* wood, *palha* is also known as Bolivian oak. This wood is sometimes used by cachaça producers during the maturation process. *Palho* is also known as *carvalho-da-bolivia*.

Pereira

Unlike most of the woods used for ageing cachaça, *pereira* is a flowering fruit tree commonly grown for its pears. But it is also prized for medicinal properties: its bark is employed as an external analgesic from bruises and sprains. Sometimes *pereira* is used in the making of infused cachaças. This tree also goes by the names *acarirana, pau-pereira, pau-forquilha,* and *quinarana.*

Pinheiro do Parami

Although this tree is called a *pinehiro* (pine), it is actually a member of the Araucariaceae family. Pinheiro do Parami is not used for ageing by cachaça producers. But it is sometimes harvested to make decorative cachaça casks, which if the spirit is left in it for too long will impart a pine tar aroma and character to the spirit.

Sassafrás

(*Ocotea odorifera*) *Sassafrás* was commonlay used in the flavouring of root beer and sassafras sodas until the 1960s. This native tree of southeast China is sometimes used by cachaça producers to impart a deep-brown hue as well as strong aroma and character to the spirit. *Sassafrás* also goes by the name *canela-sassafras*.

Vinhático

(*Plathymenia reticulata*) Another member of the Fabaceae family of trees that is indigenous to the Cerrado region, *vinhático* wood imparts a golden yellow hue and lowers acidity during the cachaça maturation process. *Vinhático* is also known as *vinhatico-da-mata, vinhatico-do-campo, vinhatico amarelo,* and *arranhagato.*

Yellow Ipê

(*Tabebuia chrysotricha Mart. ex DC.*) This tree of the Bignoniaceae family stands side by side with the *pau-Brasil* (Brasilwood) in national significance: it is considered to be country's national flower.

Yellow *ipê* primarily grows from Espírito Santo to Santa Catrina. Cachaça producers employ the wood from this tree to impart an orange colour and softness to the character of cachaça. Yellow *ipê* also goes by the names *pau-d'arco, peuva, peroba-*

do-campo, *ipe-da-serra, ipe-amarelo-da-serra, ipe-caboclo, ipe-mamono, pau-d'arco-roxo, ipe-rosa, ipe-roxo, ipe-tabaco,* and *ipe-amarelo.*

Tasting Cachaça

HOW TO ACHIEVE THE ESSENTIAL EXPERIENCE

THERE ARE AS MANY differences amongst unaged and aged cachaças, artisanal and industrial cachaças as there are among whiskeys and whiskies. Even though cachaça is regarded as Brasilian rum by the TTB (US Alcohol and Tobacco Tax and Trade Bureau), there are readily perceptible differences to be found in cachaças. Perceiving these differences is actually more a matter of training than talent.

OPPOSITE PAGE:
The best way to first experience cachaça is to drink it pure and neat.

The Tasting Environment

∞

A TASTING SHOULD BE conducted in an odor-free, well-lit room that has at least one bright-white surface (a table, a wall, or a piece of paper) that can serve as a background for viewing each spirit. Those participating in a tasting should also be odor-free: heavy perfumes, colognes, and deodorants have no place in a tasting room. Participants should not consume any strong flavors for at least thirty minutes before the tasting session. Common sense comes into play here. If you eat pizza before a tasting, you're likely to detect garlic and oregano in everything.

How to Evaluate Cachaça

You should evaluate each cachaça sample at room temperature (seventy-five to seventy-eight degrees Fahrenheit), and at full strength. If you don't have a set of Reidel Small Batch Bourbon glasses, which are shaped like smallish, short-stemmed white wine glasses, any standard white wine glass will work. First, make sure the glass is clean and free of odors. Soap residue, or even a bleached drying cloth can throw off the aroma and the taste.

Pour about 1 ounce (30 ml) of cachaça into the glass. Then, one-by-one, follow the sensory evaluation steps in this exact order: sight, smell, taste, and touch.

Sight

Hold the glass in front of a bright-white background. Check that your sample is dust-free and particulate-free. Assess the color. Does it have a silvery cast or a pale yellow hue? If it is aged, is it deep golden or dark as caramel?

Swirl the cachaça around the glass. Swirling serves two purposes. It opens up the aroma by radically increasing the surface-area-to-volume ratio of the cachaça in the glass. It also allows you to judge the glycerol content. As the cachaça sinks back into the glass, look for a thick appearance that gives you an indication of how the cachaça will rest on your tongue: will it be viscous or thin?

> With cachaça there is a unique scent: the aroma of sugar cane, vegetals, fruits, minerals, and flowers.

Some authorities say that if the liquid streams down the sides of the glass in a rosary-bead chain of small drops, it has a higher alcohol level. The bigger the beads, the weaker the spirit.

Smell

Open your mouth slightly when you bring the glass up under your nose. Then inhale. This allows the aroma to swirl across the top of your palate, where it reaches additional receptors. Now try smelling the cachaça with your mouth closed. You'll soon discover that open- and closed-mouth tasting are almost as radically different as having a cold or not having a cold.

With cachaça there is a unique scent: the aroma of sugar cane, vegetals, fruits, minerals, and flowers. Aged cachaças introduce new fragrances, such as cereals, woods, caramels, spices.

Be vary wary of tasting a cachaça that has the distinct aroma of nail polish remover or paint thinner. This indicates a high level of undesirable aldehydes in the spirit.

Taste

Just like wine, cachaça should be "chewed". Slosh the cachaça around in your mouth and draw air in across it to release the full flavor. After you've given it an initial chew, bring the glass back up to your nose to round out the flavor experience. Some purists may balk at this. However, the idea is not to separate taste and smell, but to gain the fullest possible sensory experience of the product. Now judge the taste three ways: on its composition; on its intensity; and on its duration.

Just like wine, cachaça should be "chewed".

Touch

Most people tend to forget that this fourth sense is also involved in sensory evaluation. The cachaça's mouthfeel can reveal points of quality, which aren't as apparent in its aroma or taste. A burning alcohol feel is a perfect example. A viscose texture is another. Is the cachaça thin and astringent? Or does it coat the palate?

The most essential tool for cachaça tasting (and for any other beverage tasting), is a descriptors list. Professionals commonly use lists like this to taste wine, spirits, even beer. A printed list of these adjectives allows you to quickly select appropriate flavor terms rather than trying to remember words while you should be concentrating all your efforts on analyzing the flavor.

FRUIT FLAVOURS:

Acai (a sharp, tart berry)
Acerola (rose hip)
Apple
Apricot
Baked apple
Banana
Black cherry
Blackberry
Blueberry
Boysenberry
Cacao (fresh)
Caju (cashew fruit)
Cherry
Cranberry
Cucumber
Current (red, black, cassis)
Fig
Green apple
Guava
Kiwi fruit
Mango
Nectarine

Passion fruit

Peach

Pear

Persimmon

Pineapple

Plum

Pomegranate

Prune

Quince

Raisin

Raspberry

Strawberry

Watermelon

SWEET FLAVOURS

Beeswax

Burnt sugar

Butter (fresh, rancid)

Butterscotch

Cacao bean (cocoa, chocolate)

Caramel

Cream

Crème brulée

Honey

Molasses

Powdered sugar

Toffee

Vanilla

EARTHY FLAVOURS

Chalk

Clay

Dust

Earth
Flint
Limestone
Mineral
Moss
Mushrooms (porcini, oyster, shitake)

FLORAL FLAVOURS

Grass (fresh cut, dry, hay)
Herbaceous (thyme, oregano, sage, tarragon)
Lavender
Lilies
Orange blossoms
Rosemary
Roses
Violets

VEGETAL FLAVOURS

Black pepper
Boiled potato
Celery
Coriander
Green pepper
Peppercorns

CITRUS FLAVOURS

Grapefruit
Lemon
Lemon balm
Lemon balsam

Lemon crème

Lemon grass

Lemon peel

Lemon verbena

Lime

Marmalade

Meyer lemon

Orange (sweet, bitter)

Orange zest

Tangerine

MINT FLAVOURS

Camphor

Eucalyptus

Menthol

Peppermint

Spearmint

Wintergreen

SPICE FLAVOURS

Anise

Cardamom

Cinnamon

Cloves

Fennel

Ginger

Licorice

Nutmeg

Tumeric

CEREAL FLAVOURS

Burnt toast

Fresh bread

Maize
Malt
Sweet corn
Toast
Yeast

NUT FLAVOURS

Almond
Cashew
Hazelnut
Walnut

TANNIC/DRY FLAVOURS

Black tea
Coffee
Espresso
Green tea
Tannin (crushed dry oak leaves)
Tobacco

WOOD FLAVOURS

Cedar
Leather
Maple
Oak (toasted, charred, fresh)
Pine
Pine nut
Redwood
Smoke, clean
Smoke, oily

CHEMICAL & MEDICINAL FLAVOURS

Acetone (nail polish remover)

Antiseptic (hospital aroma)

Burnt rubber

Iodine

Isopropyl (rubbing alcohol)

Electrical fire (smoky burn)

Plastic

Quinine

Sulphur

MOUTHFEEL

Astringent

Crisp

Dry

Greasy/oily

Metallic

Sparkling

Thick

Warmth or burn

WHEN CONDUCTING a tasting, remember to focus on personal acuity. Full strength cachaça has an anesthetic effect on your taste receptors. Even if you're spitting and rinsing between samples, even if you're allowing enough time between each sample for your taste receptors to recover, eventually your senses will become dulled over the course of the

tasting session. This is not a problem if you're tasting only one or two cachaças.

But if you are tasting more than that, fill a mug
with coffee beans or ground coffee. Sniff it occasion-
ally between tastings to revive your senses.

After you've finished this clinical step-by-step
sampling, there are two crucial tests for cachaça.
Since it is unlikely to be consumed at full strength
and room temperature, you need to try each cachaça
in your session both chilled and mixed in a cocktail
or mixed drink.

Lastly, always take notes. A
tasting session provides so many
details all at once. It would be impos-
sible to remember them all even if
your weren't drinking.

...you need to try
each cachaça in
your session both
chilled and mixed
in a cocktail or mixed
drink...

Classic Cachaça Drinks

AND A FEW NEW TWISTS

THE BEST INSPIRATION for developing new drinks made with a particular spirit is to look at classic long and short drinks. Classics are classics because they have broader, stronger appeal than drinks developed to suit a short-lived trend. Classics are sometimes varied because public palates change through the years; some ingredients are not as readily available in a given region; or because a mixologist researched and discovered a new twist on the base recipe.

Once a tried-and-true recipe is mastered, it is an easy progression to enhance the flavour and

OPPOSITE PAGE:
The caipirinha was designated in 2000 as Brasil's national drink in honor of the country's discovery in 1500.

aroma of a recipe, creating variations on themes, which become entirely new concoctions.

Classic Cachaça Drinks

HERE ARE A HANDFUL of traditional Brasilian libations made with cachaça to inspire you:

Pure

The most traditional way to consume unaged or aged artisanal cachaças is to sip it neat from a fifty-milliliter shot glass. This allows the taster to savour the flavours in the fore, mid, and after in small amounts. However, this hides the nose, which is not necessary with high-quality cachaça like Sagatiba.

Martelinho

Basically, the Martelinho (meaning "little hammer") is like consuming cachaça pure. But rather than sipping it, the spirit is imbibed from a short slim glass as a shot in the same manner super-premium vodka is consumed.

Batida

Created in the early 1800s by Portugal's Queen Carlota Joaquina while the royal Portuguese court resided in Rio de Janeiro during the Napoleonic Wars, the batida is a mixed drink made with cachaça, fruit juice or purée, sugar, and sometimes milk. Batidas can be made with combination of fruits. they can also be shaken or built. Passion fruit, coconut milk, lemon and honey, mint, and pineapple are some of the most popular flavours. Here is the basic recipe:

60 ml cachaça

110 gr fruit juice or purée

1 barspoon simple syrup

Shake over ice or mix in a blender with ice all ingredients. Pour unstrained into a collins glass.

Passion fruit is a very popular fruit flavour for batidas, using either fresh fruit or purée.

BATIDA MORANGO: Shake over ice or mix in a blender with ice 60 ml cachaça, five to seven ripe strawberries, simple syrup to taste, and 30 ml fresh lime juice.

BOMBEIRINHO: This particular—and very popular—built batida features *groselha* or gooseberry syrup. Build 50 ml cachaça and 1 barspoon of groselha syrup into a rocks glass. Fill with ice and stir.

BATIDA DE COCO: Shake over ice or mix in a blender with ice 30 ml coconut milk, 30 ml whole milk, 60 ml cachaça, and simple syrup to taste. Pour unstrained into a collins glass.

BATIDA DE MANGA: Sagatiba Global Brand Ambassador John Gakuru's recipe is as follows:

Shake over crushed ice 50 ml Sagatiba Pura, 25 ml fresh squeezed lemon juice, 25 ml sweetened condensed milk, 25 ml fresh cream, 25 ml mango purée (Funkin or similar). Pour into large tall glass. Top with crushed and garnish with a spear of fresh mango.

BATIDA DE MARACUJÁ: Shake over ice or mix in a blender with ice 60 ml cachaça with half of a passion fruit, 60 ml whole milk, and simple syrup to taste. Pour unstrained into a collins glass.

Caipirinha

The national drink of Brasil, the caipirinha (an endearing term for a "country person") is the direct descendant of the batida. This libation is also akin to the manhattan, martini, and daiquiri as it highlights the character of the main spirit ingredient. But like the martini, the word "caipirinha" has been tagged onto a number of concoctions that are, in truth, simply batidas with a trendy name.

The caipirinha was designated, in 2000, as Brasil's official drink during the five-hundredth anniversary of Brasil's discovery.

1 Brasilian lime (aka: key lime)
(or substitute half of a lime)
60 ml cachaça
2 teaspoons sugar or gomme syrup
Cut the lime half into 4 wedges. Muddle the wedges and sugar in an old-fashioned glass. Fill with ice. Add cachaça and stir to combine.

Caju Amigo

(meaning "friendly cashew") This drink features a fruit that is truly unique to South America: cashew fruit. There two ways to serve this drink, depending on the availablity of fresh cashew fruit juiec in your part of the world.

30 ml cachaça
1 slice of cashew flesh,
or 30 ml cashew juice (bottled or fresh)

METHOD 1: Build cashew juice and cachaça into a shot glass without ice. Serve up.
METHOD 2: Serve cachaça up neat in a shot glass. Place a slice of cashew flesh on the side. To consume, places the cashew slice on your tongue and chase it down with the cachaça.

On a cautionary note, if fresh cashews are available in your area, do not attempt to chew on the hard cashew fruit that tips the sweet fleshly portion. The cashew is related to poison ivy and poison oak. The shell that protects the familiar cashew nut has an enzyme that causes numbing and tingling.

Most people outside of South America are familiar with the nuts from this tree. But few realize that the fleshy portion of the cashew possesses a refreshingly succulent flavour.

Capeta or Capetão

(meaning "little demon") The cinnamon and condensed milk in this beverage make the capeta a surprisingly smooth refresher. This particular capeta recipe makes enough for four people.

200 ml cachaça

100 ml condensed milk

100 ml whole milk

guarana powder

ground cinnamon

Thoroughly blend the condensed milk, whole milk, and cachaça in a pitcher. Pour into tall shot glasses. Stir in guarana powder and cinnamon to taste. Let the mixture rest for a few minutes to allow the cinnamon and guarana time to open to full flavour. Serve neat.

Capeta and Leite de Onça (*see below*) are close cousins to a very popular concoction served in Puerto Rico during Christmas holidays called coquito. But these recipes are much easier to prepare and serve for a small group of people.

El Draque

(meaning "the dragon") Legend tells us El Draque was invented by pirate Richard Drake in honor of his captain Sir Francis Drake, who was nicknamed "El Draque" by the Spanish and Portuguese whose Caribbean and South American ports he and his fleet raided during the late 1500s.

Similar to the caipirinha, the El Draque is reputed by many historians to be the parent of the rum-based quencher, the mojito.

30 ml aged cachaça
6 to 8 yerba buena mint leaves
(spearmint can be used as a substitute)
1 Brasilian lime (aka: key lime)
(or substitute half of a lime)
1 barspoon turbinado or demerara sugar
Cut the lime into 4 wedges. Muddle the wedges, mint, and sugar in an old-fashioned glass. Fill with ice, Add cachaça and stir to combine.

Leite de Onça

(meaning "jaguar milk") Leite de Onça and Quentão are the drinks traditionally served during Festas Juninas, a multi-day winter feast that was originally associated with the pagan summer solstice festival of pre-Christian Europe. When the festival was imported to Brasil, it was associated with the feast days of four major Roman Catholic saints. The celebration days are the feasts of St Anthony (13 June), St John (24 June), St Pedro (29 June), and St Marçal (30 June).

Similar to Capeta, Leite de Onça is a creamy but refreshing thirst quencher.

50 ml cachaça
50 ml whole milk
50 ml crème de cocoa

25 ml condensed milk

Thoroughly blend the condensed milk and
the milk in a ceramic mug or tumbler. Add
cachaça and let it rest for a few minutes.
Add the crème de cocoa and garnish with
ground cinnamon or chocolate powder.

Licores

(meaning "liqueurs" or "cordials") More than
many other spirits, cachaça is used as the base for
flavourful homemade liqueurs. Traditionally, these
concoctions were prepared by noble women and
decanted into crystal vessels for serving to guests.
Throughout Brasil, restaurants frequently offer
homemade liqueurs as digestifs.

Honey is an extremely popular liqueur ingredient cmmon to Minas Gerais as is one made with
jabuticaba (Brasilian grape tree fruit). Pineapple,
mint, cherry, figs, peanuts, and fresh cocoa are also
crafted into liqueurs. The basic recipe is this:

470 ml fresh fruit, chopped

1 litre cachaça

120 ml simple syrup

Steep fruit and cachaça in an air-tight
glass jar for at least one week. Strain and
add simple syrup. Bottle in a decanter
and age for one month.

Quentão

(meaning "hot stuff") Quentão is another
beverage that is traditionally served during Festas

Juninas, the multi-day winter feast that takes place during the feasts of St Anthony (13 June), St John (24 June), St Pedro (29 June), and St Marçal (30 June). (Remember: Brasil is south of the equator, so winter takes place between June and August.)

This particular beverage is served piping hot with a citrus garnish, similar to a hot toddy.

2 fresh ginger roots, peeled
and cut into thin slices
2 large unpeeled red apples,
cored and cut into cubes
900 gr white granulated sugar
10 whole cloves
5 cinnamon sticks
470 ml cachaça
940 ml water

Place the ginger, apple and the sugar into a deep pan, constantly stir and cook slowly under low heat until everything caramelizes to a dark brown color. Add the cloves and the cinnamon sticks and mix a bit more. Remove the pan from the burner and mix in the cachaça. The caramelized sugar mixture will harden when the cachaça is added. Return the pan to the burner and cook slowly until the cachaça is mixed with the sugar. Add the water and simmer slowly for about fifteen minutes. Strain into mugs and garnish with orange or lemon slices or peel.

Rabo-de-Galo

(meaning "cock tail") A Brasilian sweet martini-style cocktail, Rabo-de-Galo blends two influences that have married well together for over a century: Brasilian and Italian culture.

100 ml parts cachaça
50 ml Italian sweet vermouth
Shake ingredients over ice and strain into
large shot glasses, served neat.

VARIATION I: In São Paulo, some people substitute the vermouth with Cynar, a fresh Italian bitter apéritif wine flavored with artichoke.

VARIATION II: Sagatiba's global brand ambassador John Gakuru adds campari to his version.

And a Couple Inspired Twists

∞

REMEMBER we were saying that classics such as the drinks we just presented can serve as the finest inspiration for the creation of new concoctions? Here are a few selections to prove our point:

Aman Snow Leopard

Following the inspiration of Leite de Onça and Capeta, this cocktail features the smooth marriage that can be achieved between cachaça and cream. This particular version was created by John Gakuru.

45 ml Sagatiba Pura

10 ml amaretto

3 drops of rose water essence

1 shot of espresso

Stir Sagatiba and amaretto in a mixing glass filled with cubed ice. Strain into a stemmed cocktail glass. Layer the cream on top with the drops of rose water. Draw the "S" with drops of espresso on the top of the cream.

Capiriniha Jellies

Three different classics combine in this lively creation. Naturally, the first inspiration was the caipirinha. The second comes from the cachaça jellies that are traditionally served with espresso in some regions of Brasil. The third comes from a punch jelly created by chef Alexis Benoit Soyer for his Universal Symposium of All Nations restaurant which opened in London in 1851.

360 ml Sagatiba Velha

juice of 4 Brasilian limes or 2 regular limes

120 ml simple syrup

12 leaves or 4 envelopes of gelatin

240 ml boiling hot water

Dissolve the gelatin in boiling hot water in a container. Stir in simple syrup and lime juice. Then stir in cachaça. Pour into a shallow glass baking dish and refrigerate for at least 3 hours, preferably overnight. Cut into small squares. Turn a champagne coupe or cocktail glass upside down. Place a thin slice of lime on the base and then top with 3 squares of jelly, garnished with a lime twist.

VARIATION: Cut into small squares and dust with superfine granulated sugar. Serve a cup of espresso with a square of jelly on the side.

Dumont

Sagatiba US brand ambassador Jamie Terrell named this cocktail after Brazilian aviation pioneer Santos Dumont. It takes its inspiration from both the rabo-de-galo and the aviation.

50 ml Sagatiba Pura
25 ml freshly squeezed lemon juice
12.5 ml maraschino liqueur
6.25 ml crème de mure
Shake ingredients over ice and fine strain into a frozen cocktail glass. Garnish with a fresh morello cherry on stem.

Now it's your turn.

Cachaça Food

AND THE MUSIC THAT GOES WITH IT

CUISINE AND MUSIC in Brasil are just as rich and unique as the rest of this diverse South American culture. The food repertoire ranges from sumptuous marinated meats and sausages barbecued on spits to a hearty bean-and-meat stew that rivals the finest French casoulet to simple tapas that highlights subtle flavours, especially when paired with the finest cachaças, batidas, and caipirinhas.

Brasilian music marries the best of many cultures, from African to European to Caribbean to home-grown Brasilian. Pulsating, haunting, gyrating, ecstatic. The samba delivers it all, suiting every sentiment and occasion.

Why all this talk about food and music? Because there is no better way to appreciate the soul of a country than through its food, music, and drink.

Brasil's Cuisine

Churrasco

EARLY SETTLERS IN BRASIL were the first Europeans to raise cattle in South America, importing them from the Cape Verde Islands in the 1530s. The gaúchos who raised ths particular breed of livestock developed *churrasco* (pronounced shoo-RAS-ko): lightly-salted meats skewered onto metal spits and barbecued over a pit of hot coals. Each gaúcho toted his own churrasco knife for slicing off pieces of meat straight off the spit.

Churrasco, like cachaça, is garnering a great deal of interest outside of South America. Over the centuries *churrascarias* have made their way from the ranches of southern Brasil to the fashionable neighbourhoods in Rio de Janeiro and São Paulo to American metropolises such as New York and Chicago to the cosmopolitan capitals of London and Paris.

What makes this cuisine so alluring is that preparation is kept to a minimum. And the results are so delectible. Red meats are seasoned only with coarse sea salt. Poultry and pork are marinated in garlic, lime juice, and salt. A rotisserie-style grill best replicates the slow-cook effect of the gaúcho's coal pits.

As we learned when we experienced our first churrasco in Rio de Janeiro's Leblon district, accompaniments can include a salad of fresh tomatoes and hearts of palm, fried yucca, *farofa (see below)* plus caipirinhas, batidas, and pure cachaça, of course.

Feijoada

Brasil's national dish, *feijoada*, is a little more difficult to replicate outside of South America. We might be a little prejudiced about this dish: we savoured our first *feijoada* at the Jockey Club in Rio de Janeiro on a stormy Saturday afternoon.

Feijoada was born from the kitchens of slaves, who slow-cooked the pork meats in a huge pot of black beans. Eventually the dish evolved to include side dishes of fresh orange wedges, rice,

A meat and bean stew that is cherished as much as the French love casoulet, *feijoada* is savoured by Brasilians of all social classes.

chopped scallions, and *farofa* (toasted manioc flour known as *farinha de mandioca torrada* fried in butter or oil with onion, scallion, chopped bacon and parsley). Don't forget the caipirinha apéritif and cachaça.

Want to give it a try? British super chef Jamie Oliver came up with a delectable variation that we've adapted for you to conjure up at home:

400 gr dried black beans
400 gr salt pork
400 gr salt bacon
8 tablespoons olive oil
2 onions, finely chopped
6 cloves garlic, finely chopped
2 large smoked chorizo, cut into chunks
400 gr smoked pork ribs, cut into chunks
400 gr smoked bacon, cut into chunks
1 tablespoon fresh ground black pepper
5 bay leaves

Soak the beans in cold water overnight.
In a separate pot, soak the salt pork and salted bacon.
The next day, drain the beans and put them into a large saucepan of cold water. Bring to a boil over a medium heat, then simmer for 30 minutes until tender.
Thoroughly rinse the soaked salt pork and bacon. Add to the beans and cook for 30 minutes.
Heat olive oil in a very large saucepan.
Add onions and garlic and cook until soft.

Add sausages, smoked ribs and bacon,
pepper and bay leaves. Pour into the
bean and meat mixture. Top up with water.
Simmer for about 1 hour, until the meat falls
off the bone.

Picadinho

Brasilians have their version of the French bistro, the British pub, and the Italian caffé: the *botequim* or *boteco*. A place to socialize with friends over cachaça, beer, light dishes, sometimes even music, the botequim is the center of each and every Brasilian neighbourhood.

A typical *botequim* menu somewhat resembles a Spanish or Basque tapas menu: grilled sausages, salt cod fritters, puffy pillows of meat or fish wrapped in a short pastry crust called *empandinhas*. However, there is another standard dish that tickled our fancy when we encountered it in a crowded Belo Horizante *boteco* that sported a bossa nova lounge upstairs: *picadinho*. Here is a simplified version of the recipe we tasted that featured the sun-dried beef that is a staple in Bahia.

400 gr filet mignon, coarsely chopped
1 medium onion, finely chopped
2 cloves garlic, minced
2 tablespoons sunflower oil
1 tablespoon tomato paste
salt and pepper to taste
farofa (see recipe)

Sauté onion and garlic until soft in a large pan. Add the beef and brown. Then add tomato paste. Cook over medium heat for about 3 minutes. Turn off the heat and toss with *farofa*. Serve.

Farofa:
4 tablespoons butter
3 cups manioc flour (farinha de mandioca)
salt to taste
Melt the butter in a heavy skillet. Add the manioc flour and sauté over low heat until golden, stirring constantly. Sprinkle with coarse sea salt.

Now for the musical interlude.

Brasil's Music: Samba

BRASIL'S NATIONAL MUSIC, samba, originated with two distinct influences. The first are the circles dances performed by Angolans and Congolese, who were transported as slaves to Brasil from the Sixteenth to the Nineteenth Century. The second influence was European classical music imported by emigrants from Portugal and Italy during the Nineteenth Century.

Emerging from the *favelas* of Rio de Janeiro during the early Twentieth Century, samba has evolved over the course of a century. Where do you start listening?

Get an overview by locating copies of David Byrne's *Brazil Classics, Volumes 1* and *2* compilations, which feature a few samba styles. If you want to delve further, begin by acquainting yourself with songs written by Carlos Cachaça and Carlota. Find works by Pixinguinha and João da Bahiana. Then explore the *samba de enredo* that is played at carnaval. Delve into the guitar-oriented *samba-cancon*, which led to bossa nova hits such as Tropicália artists João Gilberto and Antonio Carlos Jobim's "Girl from Ipanema" and the music featured in the 1959 French film *Black Orpheus*.

Cartola returns in samba works created during the 1960s along with artsits such as Velha Guarda da Portela and Clementina de Jesus. The next decade of this hypnotic sound features names such as Clara Nunes and Beth Carvalho.

A new form of samba appeared in the 1980s called *pagode* that employed a lot of Rio slang. Find works by Zeca Pagodinho, Grupo Fundo de Quintal, and Jovelina Pérola Megra and note that banjo and tan-tan are introduced into the samba lineup.

Samba never stagnates. Samba-reggae, a pop-style samba orginating in Bahia, appeared in 2001, adding calypso and mambo to the cross-influences samba's repertoire. Now, rap and hip-hop are being consumed into this auditory anthropophagy.

CHAPTER ELEVEN

Cachaça Today

DESPITE its tumultuous ups and downs in popularity during its nearly four centuries of existence, cachaça is as much or more a part of Brasilian culture today as vodka is to the Russians, whisky to the Scots, gin to the Brits, and tequila to Mexicans. Cachaça is an integral element in Brasil's history, its tradition, its heritage, and its identity.

Just as in colonial times, Brasil has once again become the world's largest producer of sugar cane and its derivatives. According to a 2001 Global Information Network report, one million Brasilians grew 291 million metric tons of sugar cane, distilled sixteen billion liters of cane-based alcohol, and extracted twenty million metric tons of raw sugar.

For the first time since the 1700s, cachaça's popularity as an export has reemerged thanks to the rising popularity of the caipirinha in bars across Europe, North America, and Asia. Designated by the government, in 2000, as the official drink of the five-hundredth anniversary of Brasil's discovery, the caipirinha has breathed new life into the cachaça industry.

Similar to the mojito and the margarita, the caipirinha enjoys international success due to its cultural associations. While the mojito conveys the Caribbean lifestyle and the margarita extols Mexican culture, the caipirinha is linked with the Brasilian love of the tropical lifestyle, carnaval, and samba.

Similar to the mojito and the margarita, the caipirinha enjoys international success due to its cultural associations.

Unlike the mojito, the caipirinha's secondary ingredients are as easy to stock in bars as the margarita: sugar and limes (although key limes are the preferred fruit varietal).

And even though a true caipirinha is exclusively made with Brasilian or key limes and cachaça, the word itself has been tagged onto a number of beverages that are, in truth, batidas. Similar tagging has occurred with the term "martini" which has been placed on numerous cocktails in the past fifteen years around the world.

Wishing to capitalize on this new beverage market, Brasilian producers encountered some competition from Colombian and Martinique producers who began marketing their cane-based spirits under the name cachaça.

In an attempt to protect its industry, Brasilian President Fernando Enrique Cardoso signed a decree, in 2001, establishing cachaça as the official and exclusive name for cane alcohol produced in Brasil. But this measure failed due to a lack of clear definition.

Two years later, President Luis Inacio Lula da Silva, tightened specifications on both cachaça and the caipirinha. He sent the issue to the World Trade Organization in hopes that cachaça will gain AOC-style designation under the Trade Related Aspects of Intellectual Property Rights agreement (TRIPS). Brasil is also involved in bilateral negotiations with the European Union to ensure that the term cachaça name will only be employed on Brasilian products within its member states.

Germany represents about a quarter of the export market for cachaça, where only beer exceeds caipirinha sales in its bars. Based on a percentage of total export, the world's top ten cachaça importing countries are:

> Germany represents about a quarter of the export market for cachaça...

1. Paraguay   28.19 percent
2. Germany   23.31 percent
3. Italy   6.09 percent
4. Uruguay   5.94 percent
5. Portugal   5.68 percent
6. Bolivia   4.28 percent
7. United States 4.13 percent
8. Chile   3.69 percent

| 9. | Spain | 3.60 percent |
| 10. | Netherlands | 2.39 percent |

Since 2000, exports of cachaça have sky-rocketed as a result of successful international marketing and export campaigns. According to the Brasilian Cachaça Development Program (PBDAC), 500,000 liters of cachaça were sent abroad in 1995. By 2001, 11.1 million liters were exported. That figure increased to twenty million liters distributed to sixty countries by 2003. It is anticipated that by the end of the decade, export sales could reach forty million liters.

But the real market is still at home, where 1.3 billion liters were distilled in 2001, with exports representing only one percent of that figure. PBDAC claims that there are 30,000 cachaça manufacturers producing 5,000 different brands. Of those producers, Industrias Muller de Bebidas ranks number one. Their most popular industrial cachaça, Pirassununga 51, makes up thirty-three percent of the market share alone.

Sagatiba's Role in Cachaça's Recent History

THE NAME "Sagatiba" combines the Norse word *saga*, meaning "legendary search" and the Brasilian Tupi-Guarani word *tiba*, meaning "boundless", "repeatedly", or "infinite".

Sagatiba was founded in 2003 and launched in 2004 by Marcos Moraes, who noticed the caipirinha was gaining international popularity while he was on holiday in the Mediterranean. Moraes established Sagatiba with the philosophy that both the domestic and international markets would be receptive to a cachaça of exceptional quality.

Major advances have been made over the past few decades to the cachaça distillation process, and in this field Sagatiba is an industry leader. Sagatiba uses multi-distillation (up to five times distilled) to highlight the distinctive flavor of its cachaça while stripping away any flavors that could detract from the drinking experience.

THE SAGATIBA PROCESS begins with a basic distillation of fresh cane juice, pressed from freshly cut unburned cane and then immediately fermented prior to distillation. With this process only a few days pass from the time the cane is cut to its first distillation.

Next, the raw spirit is thoroughly tested and analyzed. No amount of refinement can transform a less-than-stellar base spirit into a great cachaça. Many batches are rejected at this point. Those that pass inspection are blended with mineral water from the Guarani Aquifer, one of the world's purest and least accessible water sources.

The spirit is then "polished" in a state-of-the-art column still under the watchful eye of master distiller Nahor Gustavo Lanza Luz de Faria, who is considered one of the country's top cachaça specialists and the only Brasilian member of the American Distilling Institute. This state-of-the-art still precisely separates the various elements found in the blended cachaça so that Gustavo has complete control over each component of the finished cachaça he produces. This way he can assure that all of the desirable characteristics are retained.

After distillation, nothing is added to Sagatiba cachaça. However, the final product is subjected to a final battery of tests before it is bottled.

CANE VARIETIES used in the making of cachaça are selected not so much for flavor but for compatibility with the soil and climate in a particular location. The flavor does not vary greatly between the varieties. The most important factor is the plant's ability to generate high sucrose levels.

Cane fields can be first harvested within twelve to eighteen months of planting. A field can then be re-harvested with gradually diminishing returns for another six years.

Cane fields are traditionally burnt before harvesting. This clears off the sharp leaf edges that can cut workers. It also clears the fields of other dangers to manual laborers such as snakes, spiders, and rodents. Fields are burnt from the outside corners in toward the center so that the fast-moving fires burn into each other. This causes the fires to put themselves out by starving themselves of oxygen.

Fire trucks stand by on the edges of any field being burned in case a fire runs out of control.

While cane fires emit significant quantities of carbon dioxide, the growing cane is so effective at carbon absorption that there is a net reduction in carbon where fields are grown and burnt. Where fields are not burnt the net planetary carbon reduction of sugar cane is impressively high.

Fields only need to be burnt if they are to be harvested by hand, by workers with machetes. The work of harvesting cane by cane is considered an extremely difficult and hazardous job. Laborers, working six-hour days, earn between 1,000-2,000 *reais* (about $600-1,200 US) per week.

However, heat, sharp leaves, sharp machetes, insects, and other hazards make the backbreaking job even less desirable. Then there is the danger of lung damage from the particulates. Add to this the increased carbon reduction to be gained by harvesting by machine and it is not surprising that there is a widespread movement in Brasil to phase out hand harvesting completely within the next twenty years.

Sagatiba has already done this. Sagatiba only uses unburned cane, harvested by machine. Gustavo explained that there is an eight-year program in place in Minas Gerais to re-educate and re-train the workers into other occupations prior to their jobs being eliminated.

There has been some resistance to change. For the workers it means exchanging the certainty of an unpleasant job for an uncertain but likely much better future. For sugar producers it means invest-ing in the machines that will replace the labor force. However, environmental and labor benefits aside, economics is driving the industry inexorably toward following Sagatiba in this progressive step.

Sagatiba only uses unburned cane, harvested by machine.

WHEN SAGATIBA began production, exports represented barely one percent of total cachaça sales. By com-parison, tequila makers export approxi-mately fifty percent of their product.

Focusing on both the domestic and export markets, Sagatiba has quickly grown to be avail-able in thousands of Brasilian establishments, with foreign sales accounting for over thirty percent of its total sales. Both foreign and domestic sales are growing rapidly.

Regional Names & Euphemisms for Cachaça

G RANTED, the Portuguese poet Francisco Sá de Miranda (1481-1558) referred to Brasilian sugar cane spirit as cachaça back in the 1550s. But he was rare bird indeed. During cachaça's entire lifespan, it has been referred to under numerous names, endearments and euphemisms throughout Brasil.

Even when it was first invented in 1532, cachaça was called *aguardente de caña* (meaning "burning water of cane" or "cane brandy" or "sugar cane eau-de-vie") or *vinho de caña* (meaning "sugar cane wine") or *aguardente da terra* (meaning "brandy of the earth"). During the Sixteenth Century, spirits were still a new commodity. Many times, a beverage was termed a wine, even if its proof was forty-five percent. (This confusion continnues today in parts of Asia.) Today, there are specific differences attributed to cachaça and *aguardente de caña*, which are discussed in the chapter on the making of cachaça.

Sometimes to mask its identity from tax collectors and governmental officials, cachaça was recorded as *bagaceira*, the brandy that was imported from Portugal at a very high price.

In a contract dated from the 1730s in Bahia, cachaça was referred to by the term *agua ardentes* (aka: *aqua ardens* or *aqua vitae*) or *vinhos de mel* which means "honey wine"). Both terms had been used as early as the birth of cachaça itself.

When exported for trade to West Africa, the cachaça took the name *jeritiba* or *jeritiba da terra*. But when people saw the drops streaming from the alembic still during the then-fancy-and-new distillation process, they called the spirit *pinga* ("drops). In some regions of Brasil, the term *pinga* is more commonly used than the word cachaça.

Beyond this, numerous endearments and euphemisms have been assigned to cachaça on local and regional levels. Here, we are listing only a few of terms. To see a complete list, read *Dicionário Folclórico de Cachaça* by Mário Souto Maior, which lists hundreds of other names for cachaça.

TERM	MEANING
aca	a euphemism heard in Bahia
ácido	a euphemism meaning "acid"
aço	a euphemism meaning "steel"
a-do-ó	a euphemism heard in São Paulo
água-benta	meaning "blessed water", a common euphemism heard in Sergipe and in the northeast
água-bórica	meaning "boric acid water", a euphemism for ordinary aguardente de caña
água-bruta	a euphemism, meaning "raw water"
água-de-briga	a euphemism, meaning "fight water"
água-de-caña	meaning "sugar cane water", a euphemism heard in Sergipe
águas-de-setembro	meaning "waters of September", a euphemism heard in São Paulo
água-pe	a euphemism heard in São Paulo
água-prá-tudo	a euphemism heard in Sergipe
água-que-gato-ñao-bebe	meaning "water the cat won't drink", a euphemism heard in São Paulo
água-que-passarinho-não-bebe	meaning "water that birds won't drink", a euphemism heard in Bahia, São Paulo, and Pernambuco
água-raz	a euphemism heard in Sergipe
alicate	meaning "pliers", a euphemism heard in São Paulo and Sul
amarelinha	meaning the diminutive of "it lands on the water", a euphemism heard in Santa Catarina
amorosa	a euphemism used in Bahia, meaning "lover"
anigico	a euphemism heard in Sergipe
aninha	a euphemism heard in the north, meaning "it nestles"
apaga-tristeza	a euphemism, meaning "deletes sadness"

TERM	MEANING
aquela-que-matou-o-guarda	a euphemism heard in Pernambuco and Nazona da Mato, meaning "the one that killed the policeman"
arrebenta-peito	a euphemism heard in Santa Catarina
assovio-de-cobra	a euphemism heard in Pernambuco
azeite	a euphemism, meaning "oil"
azuogue	a euphemism heard in Minas Gerais
azuladinha	a euphemism heard in Alagoas
azulina	a euphemism, meaning "bluish"
azulzhina	a euphemism heard in the north, Santa Catarina, Estado de Rio Nordeste
baronesa	a euphemism, meaning "baroness"
bicarbonato-de-sóda	a euphemism heard in Bahia, meaning "bicarbonate of soda"
bicha	a euphemism heard in Céara, Pernambuco, and the northeast, meaning 'wormy"
bicho	a euphemism heard in Pará, meaning "animal"
bico	a euphemism, meaning "peak"
biranaite	a euphemism heard in Bahia
birnata	a euphemism used in Sergipe
birrada	a euphemism heard in Bahia
bitruca	a euphemism used in Santa Catarina
boa	a euphemism heard in Estado de Rio and Céara, meaning "good"
borbulhante	a euphemism heard in Sergipe
branca	a euphemism, meaning "white"
branquinha	a euphemism heard in the north and northeast
brasa	a euphemism, meaning "live coal"

TERM	MEANING
cachorro-de-engenheiro	a euphemism, meaning "the engineer's dog"
caéba	a euphemism heard in the north-east
café-branco	a euphemism heard in Maran-hão, meaning "white coffee"
calibrina	a euphemism heard in Rio de Janeiro
camarada	a euphemism heard in Pará
caña	a euphemism, meaning "cane" or "sugar cane"
candida	a euphemism heard in Sergipe and Estado de Rio
canha	a euphemism used in Rio Grande do Sul and Pernambuco
caninha	a euphemism that is the diminutive of caña
capote-de-pobre	a euphemism heard in Bahia, meaning "poor man's coat"
marvada	the feminine form of the term mal-vada, meaning "the evil" or "the meanie"
mardita	the feminine form of maldita, meaning "the damned"
mé	a colloquialism of the word mel, meaning "honey", because it sweetens life
tiquira	a misnomer that actually is the name for a fermented beverage made from manioc

A

Africa 40, 42, 43, 44, 47, 58, 60, 72, 106, 108, 175
aguardente 52, 57, 73, 81, 115, 174, 175, 176; *de caña* 52, 73, 115, 174, 175, 176; *de caña adoçada* 115
aguardiente de agave 50
alchemist 11, 19, 21, 22, 26
alcohol 13, 14, 77, 96, 97, 127, 133; alcoholic beverages 16, 58, 59
alembic 19, 20, 27, 52, 53, 114, 175
Alexander the Great 16, 104
al ghol 13
al kohl 13
al kol 13
Aman Snow Leopard 155
American Revolution 69
anhydrous alcohol 96, 97
Anthropophagy Movement 83, 88, 99
aqua vitae 21, 23, 24, 27, 29, 30, 31, 51, 175
Arab 13, 18, 19, 20, 23; Arabic 13, 14, 18, 21, 24, 25, 31
Aristotle 16, 17
arkhi 14
arrack 35, 38, 40, 51
Asia 16, 33, 34, 35, 40, 41, 42, 45, 54, 60, 76, 89, 103, 108, 165

B

Bacon, Roger 25, 26, 27, 30, 53
bagaceira 48, 54, 57, 66, 175
Bahia 46, 62, 65, 76, 84, 125, 128, 161, 163, 175, 176, 177, 178
bandeirantes 64, 65
bandeiras 64
Barbados 54, 93, 110, 111
batida 73, 147, 148
Benjamin Da Costa 111
beverage 16, 48, 49, 50, 54, 55, 58, 59, 165
Black Orpheus 98, 163
Black Plague 29
blocos 85
Bomebeirinho 147
boteco 161
botequim 161
brandy 48, 57, 59, 126, 140, 174, 175
Brasil 5, 6, 7, 33, 40, 43, 44, 45, 46, 49, 50, 53, 54, 56, 57, 58, 60, 62, 63, 64, 65, 66, 67, 68, 69, 70, 71, 72, 73, 74, 75, 76, 77, 78, 79, 80, 81, 83, 84, 89, 90, 91, 93, 94, 96, 97, 100, 101, 106, 107, 108, 111, 113,

114, 118, 119, 120, 121,
122, 124, 126, 130, 145,
148, 149, 151, 152, 153,
155, 157, 158, 159, 162,
164, 165, 166, 172, 174;
Brasilian 5, 6, 7, 33, 40,
43, 44, 45, 46, 49, 50, 53,
54, 56, 57, 58, 60, 61, 62,
63, 64, 65, 66, 67, 68, 69,
70, 71, 72, 73, 74, 75, 76,
77, 78, 79, 80, 81, 82, 83,
84, 85, 86, 88, 89, 90, 91,
92, 93, 94, 95, 96, 97, 98,
99, 100, 101, 106, 107,
108, 109, 111, 113, 114,
115, 118, 119, 120, 121,
122, 124, 126, 127, 128,
130, 133, 145, 146, 148,
149, 151, 152, 153, 154,
155, 157, 158, 159, 161,
162, 164, 165, 166, 167,
169, 170, 172, 173, 174
Brasilwood 44, 45, 130
Britain 24, 55, 70, 71, 75, 77;
British 25, 26, 30, 45,
54, 59, 60, 61, 62, 65, 69,
71, 72, 74, 75, 77, 78, 79,
89, 107, 110, 160, 161
brum 54
brusle ventre 112

C

Cabral, Pedro Álvares 43,
44, 46
cachaça 6, 7, 32, 33, 48, 51,
52, 53, 54, 55, 56, 57, 58,
59, 60, 61, 62, 63, 65, 66,
67, 68, 69, 72, 73, 77, 79,
81, 82, 84, 86, 87, 88,
93, 96, 97, 98, 99, 100,
103, 109, 110, 113, 114,
115, 116, 117, 118, 120,
121, 122, 123, 124, 125,
126, 127, 128, 129, 130,
133, 134, 135, 136, 137,
142, 143, 146, 147, 148,
149, 150, 151, 152, 153,
154, 155, 156, 158, 159,

160, 161, 164, 165, 166,
167, 170, 171, 173, 174,
175; artisanal 113, 114,
118, 119, 120, 133, 146;
Cachaça Defense Plan
96, 97; industrial 77, 82,
90, 113, 114, 119, 120,
133, 167
Cachaça, Carlos 86, 87, 163
cagaça 55
caipirinha 6, 100, 145, 148,
151, 155, 160, 165, 166,
169
Caju Amigo 149
Canary Islands 41, 46, 106
Capeta 150, 151, 155
Capetão 150
Cape Verde Islands 41, 42,
43, 106, 158
Caribbean 46, 48, 50, 54, 58,
60, 61, 62, 65, 106, 107,
108, 110, 111, 151, 157,
165
Carlota Joaquina, Queen 73,
77, 146
cauim 49, 55
Central Mills Project 77, 78
churrasco 158
cimarrones 61
Clement V 22, 23
coffee 76, 77, 81, 94, 142,
178
Columbus, Christopher 42,
46, 106
cordöes 85

D

de Sousa 45, 46, 48, 52, 64,
106; Martim Afonso 45,
46, 48, 52, 64, 106
de Ville-Neuve, Arnaud 21,
22, 23, 24, 25, 26, 27,
30, 53
Diaz, Bartolomeo 42, 43
Diocletian 18
Dioscorides 18, 105
distillation 13, 14, 16, 17,
19, 20, 21, 22, 24, 26, 27,

31, 32, 38, 53, 55, 96, 97,
111, 112, 113, 114, 115,
116, 120, 123, 170, 171,
175; distilled spirits 28,
55, 59, 121; distilleries
52, 53, 61, 63, 65, 66,
67, 69, 97, 114; distillery
operations 67; distilling
operations 65
Doctor: Illuminatus 24;
Mirabilis 25; Subtilis 24;
Universalis 26
Dominican 26, 37
Dutch West Indies Company
110

E

eau-de-vie 22, 50, 52, 111,
112, 174; *eaux-de-vie*
31, 33, 55
Egypt 14, 16, 17, 105
El Draque 61, 150, 151
emboabas 65
enredo 88, 163
entrudo 85
Estação Primeira de
Mangueira 86

F

favela 84, 86, 88, 98
feijoada 159
fermentation 23, 49, 111,
114, 116
fermento caipira 114
Festas Juninas 151, 153
Ford, Henry 89, 90, 91, 92,
93, 94, 95
Fordlandia 89, 91, 92, 94
France 22, 23, 29, 31, 35, 36,
37, 55, 70, 73
Franciscan 24, 25
fubá 114

G

garapa 128; *garapa azeda*
52
Geber 19, 21

Genoese 28, 29, 30, 34, 39,
40, 42, 51
Gil, Gilberto 99
Great Lisbon Earthquake 68
Greek 16, 18, 31, 105
guildive 112

H

Hayyan, Abu Musa Jabir 19
Henry o Navegador 41, 106
hierba buena 61
Hindus 49, 103

I

India 14, 15, 16, 17, 33, 37,
40, 42, 43, 44, 49, 52, 62,
103, 104, 105, 108
Italy 23, 30, 51, 55, 100, 162,
166

J

jeritiba 58, 72, 175
João, King 47, 52, 67, 70, 71,
73, 74, 77, 98, 163

K

khola 16
Kindi 20, 21, 23
Knights Templar 23, 36
Kublai Khan 35, 37

L

Latin 18, 21, 22, 24, 25, 31
Leite de Onça 150, 151, 155
Le Sorbonne 25, 26
Liber de Vinis 23, 27, 30
licores 152
liquor 15, 60, 67, 93, 104
Lisbon 43, 68, 71
Llull, Ramon 11, 24, 25, 26,
53

M

Magnus, Albertus 26, 30, 53
Mangueira 85, 86, 87, 88
manioc 49, 50, 55, 115, 160,

162, 178
Martelinho 146
Martinique 111, 112, 165
mescal 32, 33, 48, 50, 55
Minas Gerais 65, 66, 67, 81,
   114, 125, 126, 152, 172,
   177
mint 61, 147, 151, 152;
   Cuban mint 61, 147,
   151, 152
mojito 61, 151, 165
molasses 52, 66, 69, 81, 108,
   110, 112, 116, 140
Mongol 23, 35
Moors 20, 27

N

New World 5, 32, 33, 39, 40,
   44, 46, 48, 53, 59, 61,
   103, 107, 110

O

octli 49

P

Paraguay 74, 78, 166
Parati 47, 65
perino 50, 55
Pernambuco 45, 47, 48, 62,
   63, 65, 74, 75, 110, 111,
   128, 176, 177, 178
Persia 14, 18, 19, 105
Picadinho 161
pisco 32, 33, 48, 50
Polo, Marco 35, 37, 38, 39,
   41, 54
Pope: Alexander IV 27;
   Benedict IX 22; Boni-
   face VIII 22; Gregory X
   36, 37; Innocent V 22;
   Sylvester II 20
Portugal 5, 40, 41, 42, 43,
   44, 45, 56, 63, 64, 66, 68,
   69, 70, 71, 74, 75, 76, 79,
   85, 106, 127, 146, 162,
   166, 175; Portuguese
   39, 40, 41, 42, 43, 44, 45,

47, 48, 51, 56, 57, 61, 62,
   63, 71, 72, 73, 74, 75, 84,
   85, 86, 106, 146, 151,
   174
prohibition 69, 110
Proto-Indo-Iranians 15, 49
Ptolemy Soter 17
pulque 49, 55
pure 146
puri 106, 107

Q

Queen Carlota Joaquina 73,
   77, 146
Quentão 151, 153

R

Rabo-de-Galo 154
Razi 20, 21, 22, 25, 26
Red Book of Ossory 27
rhum 48, 109, 112, 113, 117
rhum agricoles 112
Rio de Janeiro 52, 63, 65,
   70, 71, 75, 84, 86, 87,
   125, 147, 158, 159, 163,
   178
Robert of Chester 21
Roman Catholic Church 23,
   78, 84
rubber 81, 89, 90, 92, 94,
   141
Rubruquis 35
rum 33, 51, 52, 54, 55, 58,
   59, 60, 61, 62, 69, 72,
   100, 109, 110, 111, 113,
   117, 118, 120, 133, 140,
   151

S

Sagatiba 5, 6, 7, 114, 123,
   146, 154, 155, 168, 169,
   170, 171, 172, 173
samba 85, 86, 87, 88, 98,
   100, 157, 162, 163, 165
São Jorge dos Erasmos 52,
   53
São Paulo 7, 54, 57, 62, 63,

64, 65, 66, 67, 68, 69, 73,
77, 78, 81, 82, 84, 95, 97,
113, 118, 119, 120, 122,
124, 125, 127, 128, 154,
158, 176
São Vicente 45, 46, 47, 48,
62
Saracen 105
Scotus 24, 25
Secretum Secretoum 25
Secunda Magia Naturalis
25
sharkara 103
Shetz, Erasmos 52, 53
Silk Road 14, 16
slaves 54, 55, 58, 61, 63, 69,
77, 86, 111, 159, 162
somarasa 15
South America 48, 65, 68,
108, 110, 126, 149, 158,
159
Spain 21, 22, 24, 27, 41, 42,
62, 70, 105, 167
spirit 6, 13, 29, 30, 33, 35,
51, 53, 54, 55, 57, 59, 60,
61, 63, 68, 69, 99, 100,
112, 113, 114, 115, 116,
122, 123, 124, 125, 128,
129, 130, 134, 135, 136,
145, 146, 148, 170, 174,
175
suceries 47, 52, 56, 63, 66,
67, 68, 77, 107; sucery
47, 52, 56, 63, 66, 67, 68,
77, 107
sugar 15, 38, 39, 40, 46, 48,
49, 51, 52, 53, 54, 55, 58,
61, 62, 63, 65, 66, 72,
73, 76, 77, 78, 79, 81,
82, 96, 97, 98, 103, 104,
105, 106, 107, 108, 109,
110, 111, 112, 113, 114,
115, 116, 118, 120, 123,
135, 136, 142, 147, 148,
151, 153, 156, 164, 165,
172, 174, 175, 176, 178;
beet 78; cane fields 61,
113; cane juice 15, 38,

40, 46, 52, 53, 54, 55, 61,
65, 66, 72, 82, 103, 104,
105, 106, 107, 109, 111,
112, 113, 114, 115, 116,
118, 120, 135, 136, 164,
172, 174, 175, 176, 178;
Creole 106, 107; Sugar
and Alcohol Institute
96, 97

T

tafia 112
Taínos 50, 51
taqtir 19
tariff 71
tasting 5, 133, 134
tax 54, 68, 69, 76, 95, 133,
175
tree 38, 39, 45, 90, 94, 121,
124, 125, 127, 128, 129,
130, 149, 152
Tropicália 98, 99, 163
Tupinambá 49
Tupis 46, 51, 55, 63, 107,
128

U

uisce-beatha 28
uisge-beatha 30

V

Vedas 15, 103

W

water of life 22, 23, 27, 28,
51
wine 6, 12, 13, 16, 17, 20,
21, 23, 27, 28, 29, 38, 50,
52, 55, 58, 59, 60, 112,
127, 134, 136, 154, 175
wood 28, 45, 121, 122, 123,
124, 125, 126, 127, 128,
129, 130, 137, 140, 141

Y

yeast 111, 112, 114, 116,
138

COCKTAIL AND SPIRITS historians Anistatia Miller and Jared Brown have been on a spirituous journey since 1992. Traveling around the world in search of the perfect drink, this couple launched their website *Shaken Not Stirred: A Celebration of the Martini®* on Halloween night from their West End flat in Vancouver in 1995. The bestselling book by the same name set them on a path that led to the publication of *Champagne Cocktails* in 1998, scores of articles and appearances, the founding of the Museum of the American Cocktail with Dale DeGroff, and the establishment of *Mixologist: The Journal of the American Cocktail.*

Moving to London in 2007, Miller and Brown are currently director/curators of Exposition Universelle des Vins et Spiritueux, located on Île de Bendor in southern France. A "permanent encyclopaedia" of the wines and spirits industry established by Paul Ricard, EUVS is celebrating its 50th anniversary in July 2008.